D0209400

KEEPING YOUR KIDS OUT FRONT WITHOUT KICKING THEM FROM BEHIND

KEEPING YOUR KIDS OUT FRONT WITHOUT KICKING THEM FROM BEHIND

How to Nurture High-Achieving Athletes, Scholars, and Performing Artists

Ian Tofler, M.D.

Theresa Foy DiGeronimo, M.Ed.

JOSSEY-BASS
A Wiley Company
San Francisco

Jossey-Bass books and products are available through most bookstores. To contact Jossey-Bass directly, call (888) 378-2537, fax to (800) 605-2665, or visit our website at www.josseybass.com.

Substantial discounts on bulk quantities of Jossey-Bass books are available to corporations, professional associations, and other organizations. For details and discount information, contact the special sales department at Jossey-Bass.

 Manufactured in the United States of America on Lyons Falls Turin Book. This paper is acid-free and 100 percent totally chlorine-free.

Library of Congress Cataloging-in-Publication Data

Tofler, Ian
    Keeping your kids out front without kicking them from behind: how to nurture high-achieving athletes, scholars, and performing artists / Ian Tofler, Theresa Foy DiGeronimo.—1st ed.
       p. cm.
    Includes bibliographical references and index.
    ISBN 0-7879-5223-0 (alk. paper)
    1. Gifted children. 2. Child rearing. 3. Parenting. I. DiGeronimo, Theresa Foy. II. Title.
HQ773.5 .T63 2000
649'.155—dc21

                                            00–010040

FIRST EDITION
HB Printing   10 9 8 7 6 5 4 3 2 1

Contents

This book is dedicated with love to my wife, colleague, and inspiration, Lisa; to Yael, Leora, and Avital, our children; and to Ozzie and Tamara, nurturing and stimulating parents, grandparents, and friends. To all those colleagues, family members, and fellow parents whose constructive criticism was so valuable. Special thanks to coauthor Theresa DiGeronimo for her astonishing work, productivity, and motivation to complete a challenging task.

—I.T.

With love to Mick, my husband and parenting partner, and to my children, Matt, Joe, and Colleen for all they have taught me about encouraging and protecting high-achieving children.

—T.D.

Thanks to our editor, Alan Rinzler, for actively encouraging and developing this project.

Preface

As the world has become increasingly materialistic, competitive, and goal driven, the normal developmental stages, needs, and vicissitudes of childhood have come to be either more and more blurred or totally ignored. What difference has this made in our ability as super moms, dads, coaches, and teachers to develop happy and successful superstars?

Tofler and DiGeronimo's preeminent book develops reasoned approaches to the development of healthy, successful, and talented children while avoiding the potentially damaging, even deadly demands placed on the shoulders of these young people. The authors focus on the most important interaction between children and adults—an interaction that can produce wondrous foundations for childhood and adult achievements, and sometimes wondrous and disturbing disasters.

Before you get into the book, however, consider the importance that U.S. administrations from as far back as Nixon to Clinton have placed on the development of children. The White House Conference for Children in December 1970 stated, "Forum 13: strongly believes that our children must become the nation's top priority, a priority not to be reflected in many policy statements, but evidenced in measurable action. Our belief is based on the following reasons: Children are, and will continue to be, the essential element of human, social and economic propagation; since they represent our nation's present and future, this country has a vested interest in their well-being. Children either individually or collectively are unable to provide their own supportive political forces and powers. Thus, without appropriate support children merely become, if they are not already, a truly disadvantaged population."

Tofler, a true pioneer in the field of sports psychiatry, brings to us a demanding number of excellent clinical vignettes that both subtly and dynamically illustrate growing and dangerous negative parenting and coaching practices, contrasting them with healthy and empowering positive alternatives. Where is the line between appropriate encouragement and pushing too hard? In collaboration with DiGeronimo, Tofler has provided marvelous examples, suggestions, guidelines, and conclusions. Tofler and DiGeronimo do not pretend to solve the whole problem. However, like few others before them, they have created a pioneering work that defines many of the elements of this serious dilemma. They show us how to distinguish between healthy nurturing and harmful exploitation as we bring up our talented, highly talented, or even "genius" children in a family setting.

As a true scientist, Tofler does not make blanket indictments of practices that seem destructive. As much as possible he presents the context of a child's overall development and discusses the potentially productive, counterproductive, or dangerous aspects. This book is a major, timely, and scholarly yet very readable psychiatric approach to one of our children's and families' greatest assets, and to the dilemmas, challenges, and potentially destructive interactions we all face as parents and adult mentors.

Using examples that are broad and commonplace yet complex, Tofler and DiGeronimo present solutions that are dynamic and often challenging. It is clear, however, that without widespread dissemination of this information about parenting and supporting talented kids—the most challenging of human processes—the self-sacrificing and altruistic efforts of unaware or uncaring perpetrators may produce pathological results in the innocent child.

Larry Stone, M.D.
Past president, American Academy of Child and Adolescent
   Psychiatry
Clinical professor of psychiatry, University of Texas Health
   Science Center at San Antonio
Executive medical director, the Brown Schools at Laurel Ridge

Acknowledgments

We would like to acknowledge the time and expertise so graciously offered by the following professionals who encourage and protect high-achieving children every day:

Jack DiSalvo
High school baseball coach
Hawthorne, New Jersey

Fred Engh
Founder and president of the National Alliance
for Youth Sports, Florida

David Feigley, Ph.D.
Sports psychologist and chair of the Department
of Movement Science
Rutgers University, New Jersey

Lawrence Ferrara, Ph.D.
Chair of the Department of Music and Performing Arts
New York University

Lori Hendricks
Coordinator of the NCAA CHAMPS Life Skills Program
Indianapolis, Indiana

John Hodges
Director of marketing and public relations
for the Amateur Athletic Union (AAU)
Lake Buena Vista, Florida

Peter Libman
Director of student life
School of American Ballet
New York

Deborah Mitchell, D.M.A.
Director of music education
College of the Arts at California State University, Long Beach

Ralph Opacic, Ed.D.
Executive director
Orange County High School of the Arts, California

Sally M. Reis, Ph.D.
Professor of educational psychology and president
of the National Association for Gifted Children
University of Connecticut

Joseph S. Renzulli, Ph.D.
Professor of gifted education and director of the National
Research Center on Gifted and Talented Education
University of Connecticut

Peter D. Rosenstein
Executive director of the National Association for Gifted Children
Washington, D.C.

Ellen Savitz, M.Ed.
Principal
Philadelphia High School for Creative and Performing Arts

Chuck Schnabel
Director of Raising Confidence Skills Corporation
and a professional scout with the Philadelphia Phillies
Wyckoff, New Jersey

Robert Sternberg, Ph.D.
Professor of psychology and education at Yale University and
associate director of the National Research Center on Gifted
and Talented Education

Andrew Thomas
Director of precollege admissions
The Juilliard School, New York

Introduction

Keeping kids out front without kicking them from behind sounds like a great idea. We know that the world is full of parents who want to encourage their high-achieving children to strive for the gold, who want their children to attain the full promise of their potential yet also want to protect them from the tension, stress, and pressure of high parental expectations and those of relentless instructors. These parents demonstrate the ideal: the admirable goal of supportive parenting.

The reality of raising high-achieving children, however, is much more complex than this simple desire. This generation of parents wants not only to encourage and protect but also to push, push, and shove their children to the front of the line. In the process of trying to prepare our children for a rapidly evolving and fiercely competitive world, we too often professionalize and adultify our children by taking the fun out of childhood. We have turned summer camps into training camps where kids work hard to learn and improve useful skills. We have stolen lazy Saturday afternoons spent daydreaming under a tree and replaced them with adult-supervised, adult-organized activities and classes. We have taken our kids out of the neighborhood playgrounds and placed them in dance and music classes, in SAT preparation classes, and on organized athletic teams. There is no time that can be wasted on idle pastimes and no talent left unexplored or exploited.

Developing kids' talents hasn't been easy on parents either. We get caught up in keeping up with the Joneses; we sacrifice untold time chauffeuring our kids from place to place and spend incalculable amounts of money paying for their programs, equipment, travel, and instruction.

When we step back and look at this situation objectively, the question that begs to be answered is this: *Where do parents draw the line between encouraging and pushing too hard?* The purpose of this book is to provide guideposts along the road of child rearing to answer that question. We show you what defines that line between healthy nurturing and harmful exploitation. We point out the warning signs that tell you when you're about to cross over that line. And we talk about what to do to get yourself back on the healthy side if you find yourself teetering over the edge.

In Part One, we take a historical look at the relationship between parents and children. You will see that child-rearing practices believed to be "in the best interest of the child" included not only child labor in coal mines in the 1800s but also include six hours or more of daily practice for young gymnasts today. This examination of the changing concept of childhood will bring us to an introduction of what I (Dr. Tofler) and colleagues call Achievement by Proxy Distortion (or, as it is called throughout this book for short, ABPD). ABPD is a psychological state in which the parent's need for the fame, financial benefits, career advancement, or social recognition and respect that can be gained through the accomplishments of a child takes priority over the needs and goals of that child.

We explore the three stages of ABPD: (1) risky sacrifice (such as when a family moves in order to be closer to a good training facility and invests the family savings in lessons and equipment), (2) objectification (such as when a child is treated as a product to be improved and marketed rather than as a human being with needs and feelings), and (3) potential abuse (such as when a child is verbally, physically, or sexually abused because of a parent's or mentor's inability to separate his or her own needs from those of the child). Part One concludes with seven guidelines that will help all parents separate their own needs, ambitions, and dreams from their children's.

Part Two gives you the information you need to encourage and protect your children while they develop their special talents. In this program, we explore how to determine if a child is truly exceptional; how to choose classes, schools, and camps that cater to high-achieving children; and how to deal with over-the-edge instructors. We also discuss how to weigh the cost of the sacrifices that families, children, and siblings make in the pursuit of excellence. We discuss how to keep the child's adult future always in mind when making decisions that affect his or her childhood. We examine the red flags that point to ABPD trouble. And finally, we offer a method of self-analysis that will help you determine if you have fallen into ABPD traps that may be hurting your child.

Raising children who are fulfilled, healthy, sensible, and successful is not an easy task under any circumstances. The task, paradoxically, is especially difficult with young athletes, scholars, and performing artists who are blessed with exceptional gifts. These very gifts can push them into the spotlight, where they run the risk of being entitled and self-serving. Too often they become defenseless prey and even willing or colluding partners to unscrupulous parents or other adults. These children desperately need their parents to protect them, to guide them, and to nurture their whole being—body and spirit—while they strive to achieve their full potential. *Keeping Your Kids Out Front Without Kicking Them From Behind* is a step-by-step guide that will help you do just that.

PART I

An Up-Close Look at Parents and Children

Debating What Is Best for Our Children

Evolutionary theory suggests that each new generation of a robust species should have the chance to be more successful than the one that came before. All our high-achieving children put the ideas behind this theory into practice and to the test. We have every reason to expect that their lives will be better and richer than our own. In today's success-driven world, it is no longer remarkable when the unborn fetus is often exposed to "head start" stories and music; children routinely attend "Ivy League" preschools and take standardized college entrance exams at age twelve. Many begin music, dance, acting, or voice lessons at age three, and others travel the globe playing on elite sport teams by age ten. Basking in their precocious accomplishments, we as ambitious, driven, and, of course, successful parents naturally feel proud and somehow responsible for their success.

This generation of parents is brimming with good intentions. We want our children to reach their full potential and be "the best"—and we are willing to sacrifice untold time, effort, and money to make this happen. High-achieving children who find themselves successful in academics, athletics, or any of the performing arts become the brightest jewel in the family's crown. However, along with this parenting style comes the unavoidable question: Just how far should parents or adult mentors push children to ensure that they are the best? Should seven-year-old Jessica Dubroff have been allowed to commandeer her cross-country plane trip that ended in her death? Did the provocative poses taught to six-year-old Jon Benet Ramsay and her lush $500 dresses contribute to the sexualization and eventual murder of this young beauty queen? When fourteen-year-old Hannes Sarkuni, his fifteen-year-old brother Sehrope, and their fifteen-year-old cousin Shant all graduated Rutgers University before they could grow a full beard, did they lose something called childhood? When Misty Copeland moved out of her poor family home at the age of sixteen to train and live with a dancing coach and suddenly had no time to visit her mother, was she deprived of something she needed for healthy development? The "right" answers are debatable depending on one's view of the parent-child relationship, the role of peers and stability, and indeed the whole purpose and concept of childhood.

The role of the child in different societies and cultures has evolved in fits and starts throughout history and will no doubt continue to be redefined. The following broad historical overview illustrates the changeable nature of the phrase *acting in the best interest of the child.* This insight gives us a way to evaluate more objectively whether the way we encourage this generation of children to be the best is in fact in their own best interest. As you read through this book, you'll read many examples of parental decisions that were made in the supposed best interest of the child that were not always truly best for the child.

Children as Sacrificial Lambs

Two thousand years b.c.e., child sacrifice was not at all uncommon. In the Bible we read that Abraham was asked to sacrifice his only son to God, and he was willing to do so. At the time, this was not an uncommon, repugnant, or culturally unreasonable request. Children have been sacrificed throughout history in religious ceremonies as well as in cultures that valued only the strongest (often male) offspring.

These sacrifices that were made in "the best interest" of the child or of the overall society are not so primitive as we'd like to think. They are not so far removed in intent from today's late third trimester abortions of children who are not wanted or are not physically ideal. Or from the infanticide (especially of female infants) routinely practiced (if not officially sanctioned) in countries like China. This is not a judgment of right or wrong; it is an observation of what is.

Children as Goods and Chattel

Throughout most of recorded history, children were considered the property of adults. They were used physically, emotionally, economically, and sexually on all socioeconomic levels without any notice or outcry. In fact, it was not until the seventeenth century that the concept of childhood was even recognized as a status separate and distinct from adulthood. Unfortunately, this recognition did not put an end to childhood exploitation. The Industrial Revolution sucked up poor children as young as five years of age, who endured long hours of brutal and dangerous factory labor. Parents defended the situation as being in the best interest of the child, citing the Puritan ethic that saw child labor as a natural blessing. Even the passage of the first Factory Act in 1802 protected only pauper and orphan children; it did nothing for those still under their parents' supervision.

A milestone in child rights occurred in 1842 in England. The seventh earl of Shaftesbury presented evidence to the House of Commons detailing the unspeakable abuse of children as young as four who were working as beasts of burden in the coal mines of England and Scotland. The "reformation" of 1842 sought to eliminate the exploitation of these children by reducing the working hours of a child under age twelve to ten hours a day. Imagine believing that working *only* ten hours a day was best for the children! But at least it was a start.

Children as Innately Evil

The trauma of being a child during the seventeenth and eighteenth centuries was further amplified by prevailing religious beliefs (particularly those held by the evangelical Protestants called Calvinists). Preachers professed that children carried the burden of original sin and must be cured of their evil inclinations in order for them to achieve salvation. At this time it was the duty of Christian parents to use sternness and whippings to purge their children of this sin. Playfulness in children was considered ominous. It was believed that children could learn to obey God only by first learning to obey their parents. The noted clergyman John Wesley admonished parents: "Break their wills that you may save their souls" (quoted in Packard, 1983). These parents were absolutely sure that severe beatings were for the children's own good.

Leaving religion aside, the notion of "spare the rod and spoil the child" persists in many homes today—but now we have a new and forbidding catch phrase: child abuse and neglect.

Children Abused

In 1896, Sigmund Freud presented a paper, titled "Seduction Theory," that caused a major public outcry. He suggested the astonishing and frighteningly original idea that sexual and physical child abuse is one of the major causes of psychological and medical symptoms of older children and adults. Freud recanted this claim within a single year, after he was subjected to enormous hostility, ridicule, and, yes, abuse by his peers in the medical profession and by the horrified general community.

Still, despite this major setback, there were signs in the late 1800s and early 1900s that adults were ready to consider the idea that children were more than property to be beaten and whipped into shape. In 1871, the Society for the Prevention of Cruelty to Children was founded with support from key members of the previously established Society for the Prevention of Cruelty to Animals. (This in itself is an ironic commentary on social priorities!) Houses of refuge were established for neglected and abused children. Some state courts created a safety net by establishing that in extreme cases, children could not be removed from the care of their parents and placed in the hands of a government institution. For the first time, society had begun to acknowledge that what parents desire for their children—and do to them—is not necessarily what is best for them.

Unfortunately, it would be another sixty-five years after the "Seduction Theory" fiasco before Kempe and colleagues presented "The Battered Child Syndrome" in 1962. The publication of this article galvanized medical, legislative, and media attention to the problem of child abuse and neglect. It led to the establishment of protective service agencies and mandatory reporting laws in all of the states.

Finally, in the last quarter of the twentieth century, society has been willing to consider the idea that children not only are more than property but also are human beings with rights who require special protection and treatment. The grudging acknowledgment of physical child abuse has led slowly to a recognition of other, less obvious forms of abuse, such as the nonorganic failure-to-thrive syndrome, chronic neglect, sexual abuse, and factitious by proxy abuse.

As the definition of abuse continues to develop, new questions arise. Is it abusive to require a thirteen-year-old musical prodigy to practice eight hours every day? Is it abusive to expect an injured athlete to compete in the championship game? Is it abusive to take play time away from academically gifted young children and enroll them in after-school and Saturday-school classes? This kind of behavioral intervention occurs across the country a thousand times a day in households where parents want only the best for their children. But history shows us that actions and decisions are not necessarily good and acceptable just because they grow from a parent's, family's, or nation's genuine desire to do what is best for the child. Witness the Elian Gonzalez case in which all individuals, groups, and even governments have cited "the child's best interest."

Children as Gold

Widespread use of the contraceptive pill after 1962 indelibly changed the relationship between parent and child. Couples now had the opportunity to choose whether or not and when to have children. Family size dramatically decreased, and the children were now wanted, planned for, and "golden." Medical care had advanced, ensuring a majority of healthy, even premature, births and complete recovery from childhood illnesses. This gave parents the freedom to attach emotionally to their children without fear of losing them.

In the early 1980s, in-vitro fertilization made it possible for more people to have "wanted" and precious children. Older, childless couples who would give the world for a biological heir were now able to conceive and bear healthy children. The time, cost, and effort required for these miracle births were rewarded with a very special child who was worth more than his weight in gold to his parents.

This new generation of wanted children is loved, pampered, and privileged. They are given all that money can buy. They are being lovingly molded into nothing but the best. This is a new variation of old parenting styles that sets up unique family dynamics and a brand new way of defining what is best for a child.

Children as Collateral

Conceiving, bearing, and raising a wanted child is not cheap. Typically, golden children enjoy economic privilege, even if their parents must sacrifice their own needs to achieve it. Money plays a crucial role in creating children who are the cream of the crop. It is expensive to hire private tutors, coaches, and instructors. Specialty schools, camps, and classes are costly and cater exclusively to "exceptionally talented" youngsters whose parents can pay the fee. With so much invested both financially and emotionally, what is the payback for parents? What does a parent get in return for years of chauffeuring a son back and forth to the city university for advanced math classes? What does a mom get for providing years of private voice, dance, and acting lessons for her daughter? What does a dad get for traveling all over the country with his son's soccer team and sacrificing his own leisure and vacation time to the playing field? Do these children owe their parents anything?

Very often, there is an implied (if not stated) debt to be paid. Many high-achieving children are held as collateral for these investments of money, time, and attention. The payback is in their willingness to sacrifice their own instincts and goals to their parent's wishes. It is in their ability to earn college scholarship money. It is in their commitment to hours of practice or study. It is in their sense of obligation to bring attention and admiration to the family. These children learn early that they owe it to their parents to become the best. Thousands of children accept this deal and open themselves to potential exploitation not only by their parents but also by coaches, mentors, and instructors. When this process occurs, is history repeating itself? Are children once again nothing more than glorified goods and chattel who are robbed of childhood in the name of what's good for them?

The Line Between Encouragement and Exploitation

As we have discussed, it is clear that the relationship between children and adults evolves over time and that practices that are socially acceptable in one generation are not in another. We believe that in the twenty-first century, the exploitative abuse of high-achieving children will come into focus. As our society begins to examine the possibility that singlemindedly pushing children to be the very best has great potential for detriment to the healthy development of the person inside the child.

To examine this emerging form of potential abuse, we will need to define the difference between encouragement and exploitation. We believe the line is drawn at the point that separates the parent's needs and goals from those of the child. This book will help you determine what is truly best for your child and give you the information you need to encourage your child's potential without pushing him or her over that line.

From Benign to Abusive

There's one thing all parents have in common: we want the world for our children. There's an instinctive drive to want to give them the best, to nurture their talents, to try to open doors that were closed to us. It's normal to feel pride in their accomplishments, to feel hurt when they fail, and to make their goals a part of our own lives. What dad can watch his son hit a grand-slam home run and not feel his own heart jump for joy? What mother can watch her daughter accept top academic awards upon graduation and not feel a deep sense of satisfaction and accomplishment? These feelings are perfectly normal. They are what fuel parents' efforts to help children reach their full potential—to be healthy, successful, and sane human beings.

Although this end goal is generally the same in most families, the way parents guide their high-achieving children through the vicissitudes of childhood, adolescence, and early adulthood is certainly many and varied. Some parents stay in the background and are very low key. Others are very vocal and visibly proactive. Some are domineering, others more flexible. In fact, the range of styles parents use when dealing with a high-achieving child extends from perfectly normal to blatantly neglectful and abusive. But the line between the two is not always clear cut. There is great debate about the extent of parental involvement necessary to bring a talented child to the top.

What is required to produce a fourteen-year-old Olympic gold medalist gymnast like Dominique Moceanu? A fifteen-year-old Rachmaninoff virtuoso like David Helfgott? A twelve-year-old movie actor like Macaulay Culkin? Or a fourteen-year-old university graduate like Hannes Sarkuni? In truth, there are many factors that contribute to the development of accomplished young people, but more significant than all the others is the ambitious driving force of the parents behind these children.

At birth, the latest-model hard drive that is a child comes preloaded with multiple future talents and potential strengths that run the gamut of human experience. The child is then handed over to his or her parents, who download their own zip-drive floppies of cultural values and personal needs and imperatives. The talented child (and all children are talented in some way) can be programmed early on with the desire to make it big, to take that step further "west," and to achieve the unfulfilled goals and agendas—both the spoken and the implied—of the parents. In her book *The Drama of the Gifted Child,* Alice Miller (1979) observed, "from the very first day onward, he [the newborn baby] will muster all his resources to this end [the approval of his parents], like a small plant that turns towards the sun in order to survive." Is this normal or abnormal? Good or bad? One need not look far to see that the results of well-meaning and extremely ambitious parenting can be laudable on some levels and potentially disastrous on others.

The final results often depend on the motivation of the parents. For example:

Darrell wants his daughter to get good grades in school so that she can attend his rather selective alma mater and enjoy the same positive experiences he had.

Susan has signed her son up for voice and piano lessons because he seems to have a natural talent, because he likes to be the center of attention, and because she wants him to be a well-rounded person.

Marge and Scott support their son's love of highly competitive soccer, hoping the sport will help him develop the traits of persistence, determination, and good sportsmanship.

In all these cases, there seems to be unselfish motivation on the parents' part. It doesn't seem that the children are being used to work out the parents' thwarted ambitions or to meet obsessive vicarious goals. In cases like these, the results should be positive.

But there are some parents who see their children as their own last great hope. These parents, who are driven by a need to revive their own lost dreams or romantic fantasies, easily cross the line. Take the example of tennis parents whose public outbursts have made them courtside clowns or pariahs and who may eventually be banned from attending matches or tournaments and finally become alienated from their children. Or the stage moms whose tantrums for attention are industry legend. Or the parents who repeatedly insist that their children take honors and advanced placement courses against the sound advice of all the children's teachers and instructors. In these cases, it appears that the parents are focusing more on their own needs than on those of their children. When parents cross this line between caring for a child's welfare and caring too much for their own agenda, the results are often troublesome.

As we mentioned earlier, the type of parenting employed to raise high-achieving children can fall anywhere along a continuum between normal and abusive. Certainly children need help to reach their full potential, but there is a difference between encouragement and potentially abusive bullying. Some parents are aware of the difference; others are not.

When Things Seem to Go Right

In recent years, the nation's eyes have been drawn repeatedly to extraordinary cases of high-achieving children. Sometimes all the pieces of the story seem to fit just right. Tiger Woods, for example, who was groomed from birth for golf superstardom, emerged a symbol of intensive, early training gone right. His parents appeared to be supportive rather than stereotypically demanding. *Sports Illustrated* (1996, p. 37) told its readers, "As he took his son to the first tee of his first international tournament in second grade, Tiger's father said, 'Son, I want you to know I love you no matter how you do. Enjoy yourself.'" This attitude set the pattern for the years of tournaments to come. When Tiger was urged to go pro rather than go to college, his mom shot back, "Money can't buy us. If you turn him pro, you take his youth away from him" (1996, p. 37). Tiger Woods arrived on the pro circuit in 1996 as a confident, well-mannered, exceptionally talented phenom, winning $790,594 in eight major championships in just two months. No one can really be certain what went on in this family to produce this young superstar, and Earl Woods's autobiographical account does raise some real red flags, such as the marine techniques he used for the psychological "toughening up" of the eight-year-old Tiger that included trying to break his focus while practicing by making noise, jiggling keys, and shouting out at a moment of intense concentration. Nevertheless, today this young man is making millions of dollars doing something he apparently loves. All the pieces seemed to be in the right places.

Teen star Natalie Portman has also grabbed headlines that announce her astonishing accomplishments as an actress and her family's role in that success. At age eleven, Portman made her screen debut in *The Professional* and then went on to appear with Al Pacino in *Heat,* with Jack Nicholson and Glenn Close in *Mars Attacks!,* and with Tim Hutton, Uma Thurman, and Matt Dillon in *Beautiful Girls.* Portman graduated to marquee status with her appearance as the teenage queen of the planet Naboo in the *Star Wars* prequel *The Phantom Menace* and in her starring role opposite Susan Sarandon in *Anywhere but Here.* For the better part of a year, Portman took a break from the camera's eye to star in *The Diary of Anne Frank* on Broadway. She did all this while attending school and keeping up her A+ grade point average in advanced placement classes and gaining early acceptance into Harvard and Yale.

To make all this happen without sending Natalie down the destructive road that has lured so many young actors and actresses before her, her parents have kept a close watch that has often caused them to be characterized as invasive and overprotective. But those who have worked with the family tell a different tale. In a recent *Vanity Fair* article ("Through the Stardust," 1999), James Lapine, the director of *The Diary of Anne Frank,* says, "They're very down-to-earth people. I found them to be concerned parents, not stage parents" (p. 198). This thought is echoed by designer Isaac Mizrahi, who used Portman as the muse for his "Isaac" ad campaign. "I heard her parents were very overprotective, that they watch every single step of what she does, but when I met them I realized they were just concerned with their daughter," he says. "They value her. . . . I think that's why Natalie feels lighthearted; she feels cared for. I think her parents are doing everything right. She's sort of a miracle, that she hasn't become this egomaniacal little bitch like the kid stars you hear about" (p. 198). Natalie too sees her parents' presence in her life as a benefit. "They talk to the director for hours before every project I do to make sure I'm not going to be doing anything that's going to hurt me in my personal life," Portman says (p. 198). Even Wayne Wang, who had to rewrite a sexually explicit scene in *Anywhere but Here* to get her parents to allow Natalie to take the role, agrees: "If I had a daughter like Natalie, I would probably do exactly what her parents are doing" (p. 197).

Examples of high achievers with parents who stay on the safe side of the dividing line are not only to be found on the celebrity circuit; they are all around us:

Eighteen-year-old Renee is off to college to major in musical theater—against her parents' best advice. They would prefer she major in education or even law, but they also recognize Renee's passion for the theater and understand that she has to follow her own dreams, not theirs.

Eight-year-old Marc is a top competitor in karate, and his parents are very proud of his accomplishments. But they have resisted the instructor's insistence that Marc train six days a week. "I'm just not convinced," says his dad, "that Marc has to give up everything else in order to continue competing on a high level."

Ten-year-old Steve is a standout pitcher who brought his team to the championship tournament, in which they won first place. Shortly afterwards, he was invited to join a select traveling team for the summer. His father was disappointed and confused when his son said he didn't want to spend his whole summer playing more baseball, but the father didn't insist. Steve went on a short vacation with his friend's family as planned and then returned for two weeks of computer camp. No one mentioned the "missed opportunity" again.

Marilyn's five-year-old daughter, Kate, won a local beauty pageant, making her eligible to compete in the state pageant. When mother and daughter arrived for the first of a series of rehearsals, Marilyn was shocked. The little girls were all wearing makeup and outfits that belonged on sexy eighteen-year-olds. "The mothers were swapping stories of their daughters' dance, and voice, and music lessons," Marilyn remembers. "My first thought was that I had a lot of work to do to get my daughter ready to compete—I guess my own ego got wrapped up in the excitement of the moment. But then I looked at Kate and remembered that this wasn't about me; I had to do what was best for her. Thank goodness, I came to my senses, and with my daughter in hand, we walked out and never went back."

Jeff was popping his buttons the day his five-year-old son's teacher and principal suggested that the boy skip kindergarten and move into first grade. Jeff had always felt that his son was exceptionally smart; here was the proof. But after some thought, Jeff declined the offer. His son had been born prematurely and was physically and emotionally behind his peers. Although Jeff was personally flattered by the opportunity for his son, he knew it wouldn't be in the overall best interest of the child, who still needed time to develop.

The Secret of Achievement by Proxy

How can we raise successful, but also healthy and sane, high-achieving children? The key is in understanding a psychological behavioral continuum I (Dr. Tofler) and my colleagues call the *Achievement by Proxy* (ABP) spectrum. Underlying this idea is the fact that almost all parents strongly identify or empathize with their children from the moment the children are born. They feel the pain of their children's setbacks and similarly experience pride, joy, and triumph in their accomplishments. ABP explains why parents encourage and derive so much pleasure from a child's milestones and achievements, such as the first smile and the first step, and the first time on the athletic playing field or on the stage. In a healthy and sane "by proxy" experience, a supportive parent or adult can vicariously experience a child's success or failure and at the same time realize that the child is a separate individual with her own unique needs and goals.

In supportive ABP situations, financial and social benefits from a child's success are not the adults' primary goal. These collateral benefits are no more than a pleasant side effect. The child or adolescent's individuality is acknowledged, and the involved adults have the ability to distinguish the child's needs and goals from their own. ABP is normal, healthy, and sane.

Achievement by Proxy Guidelines

We will use the following guidelines throughout this book to keep parental involvement with high-achieving children within the normal and supportive boundaries. Each decision that you make regarding a child's special talents should be double-checked against this simple seven-point list:

- Guideline 1: *Parents should acknowledge the child as a unique individual with his or her own separate physical and psychological attributes.*
  Example: Even though a father has his heart set on having his offspring follow in his footsteps as a trial attorney, he may encourage or role model but not overtly force or even subtly pressure his child who shows potential talent but little interest or passion. The intelligent child will intuitively sense unstated parental wishes, and this father openly addressed this as well.
- Guideline 2: *Parents should be able to recognize the child's psychological and physical needs and then make and prioritize decisions based on these requirements rather than on their own wishes, ambitions, and fantasies.*
  Example: A parent who has an academically gifted child will allow the child to attend the birthday party of a good friend even though that means she might miss one Saturday class at the local college.
- Guideline 3: *Parents should be able to acknowledge and distinguish between their own feelings of anger and disappointment (as well as their pride and pleasure) and the child's feelings; they should not project their own feelings onto the child.*
  Example: A mother who is infuriated that her daughter has not been chosen to dance the lead role will keep her anger to herself and help her daughter learn how to deal with this disappointment. She will not pull her daughter out of the show and refuse to let her perform for that company because of her own (possibly justified) anger and rage.

- Guideline 4: *Children should never feel that parental love is contingent on winning or excelling in any one educational, sporting, career, or social endeavor.*

  Example: When a child wins second place rather than first place, he knows that although he feels disappointed, he can count on his parents' love and support. He is not worried that he will be punished or verbally abused for missing the highest mark.
- Guideline 5: *Parents must retain the power to make parental decisions. It is crucial that parents make tough—even courageous and unpopular—but developmentally appropriate, responsible judgments for the child.*

  Example: When the coach says a nine-year-old soccer player must attend a sleepaway camp on the other side of the country, but the parents perceive that she isn't yet emotionally secure enough to leave the family, the parents must feel confident in their right and responsibility to say no to the coach. They must be able to do this even if the stakes are high—for example, if the coach uses emotional blackmail tactics: "I will quit as the child's coach if she doesn't go."
- Guideline 6: *Parents should encourage developmentally appropriate independence, autonomy, and decision-making skills in their children. They should not, however, hide behind that independence when important, even critical, decisions are to be made.*

  Example: Parents who know that a child's developing skeletal structure should not be overstressed will not let their pre-teen baseball pitcher throw a doubleheader just because he says his arm feels good and his coach or teammates beg him to. Parents will not let a ten-year-old tennis player move into her coach's home simply because the child agrees with the wishes of the coach and it makes economic "sense." Parents will not allow a very young musician to practice eight hours a day because "she wants to."
- Guideline 7: *Social and financial benefits of the child's achievements should be a dividend rather than a primary (or even a disguised primary) goal for the adult.*

  Example: The parents of a talented young cello player will resist the temptation to enter their child in five national competitions during the summer in the hopes of winning enough prize money to take a desired vacation.

When Things Go Wrong

Unfortunately, the dark side of high achievement is ever present; sometimes things go wrong. We see it repeatedly in the sport of women's gymnastics: we all watched Kerri Strug's famous (but unnecessary) injured gold medal leap; we saw Dominique Moceanu fall on her head (and receive no immediate medical attention) at the Atlanta Olympics. Their bodies (and, some could argue, their lives) seemed of secondary importance to their results, as ambitious parents, charismatic coaches, and a proud, competitive nation urged on these young women.

What are we to think about the 1996 sexual molestation conviction of the respected and charismatic Canadian junior hockey coach, Graham James? The supportive system of parents and mentors failed Sheldon Kennedy (who went on to be a player for the Boston Bruins) and three other teens who were molested by James between 1984 and 1994. Kennedy was aware that his parents had sacrificed much to allow him to live and train with this well-respected and generally nurturing coach and mentor. He knew his success was expected in return. He has said that he couldn't tell his parents about the abuse for fear of disappointing or angering them. High-achieving people-pleasers, such as these isolated adolescent boys, with so much on the line, are particularly ripe for abuse.

A similar case is that of one of my colleagues, in which the father of a sixteen-year-old female member of the national swim team was informed by worried teammates of a sexual relationship between the coach and the man's daughter. The father did not initially want to confront either his daughter or the coach because he worried that a confrontation would jeopardize her future on the team. It was best, he believed, to remain silent. The question he really needed to answer was, Best for whom?

The problems that can plague success are not confined to athletic endeavors. In her memoir, *Forbidden Childhood,* the musical prodigy Ruth Slenczynska gave us a glimpse of the true misery that can lie behind the development of artistic talent. Ruth tells of her efforts to learn a certain Haydn sonata. Before she mastered it to the fanatical level of perfection her father demanded, she sustained an untold number of slaps, had her ears boxed, was sworn at in five languages, and was pushed violently off the piano bench. Not a moment of her life was permitted to be "wasted" in playing with dolls, skipping rope, going to a movie, riding a tricycle, or playing with other children. Yet her fame was international by the time Slenczynska was four. She was acclaimed as having "the temperament, the brilliance and the confidence of a born virtuoso" (Fisher, 1973, p. 13). Surely her father believed that despite his clearly abusive parenting practices, which included verbal and physical torture, he was successfully doing what was best for his child.

The problems that can plague success are not confined to prodigies. Many parents have turned their high achiever's childhood into a nonstop race to the top. For these kids there are no such things as leisurely weekends for hanging out, enjoying friends, and exploring life. There is now a whole generation of sixth graders taking college math classes every Saturday. Pickup ball games in the back lot have been abandoned and replaced by traveling elite teams that fly kids all over the country for weekend tournaments. Talented young dancers and musicians are tracked into intensive practice regimes that require hours of dedication daily.

In many of these cases the children are the pawns, not the players. The adults, who were supposed to guide and support the talents of high-achieving children, crossed over the line between normal, supportive parenting (ABP behavior) to abnormal, distorted parenting behavior: *Achievement by Proxy Distortion* (ABPD). An adult is exhibiting ABPD when the external benefits of the child's achievements become important, concurrent, or even primary goals for the adult, not a simple dividend of success. The potential benefits to the parents of a high-achieving child include the potential for fame, financial gain, career advancement, and social recognition and respect. When an adult puts the attainment of these benefits before the needs and goals of the child, he or she becomes capable of a unique form of child abuse and neglect.

The Psychological Roots of Achievement by Proxy Distortion

The concept of ABPD is an extension of the work of Roy Meadow, an English pediatrician. In 1977, Meadow uncovered a psychological state that he called Munchausen Syndrome by Proxy. In this state, highly engaging, intelligent, and apparently caring mothers induce illness and even death in their children to gain attention and nurturance for themselves. These moms have been known to poison their children or withhold food or medication to set the stage for a frantic rush to the hospital, where concerned doctors and nurses give the mothers the attention and sympathy they crave.

A 1994 case in Florida (which is still under litigation at the time of this writing) is an interesting example. In this case, it is suspected that the mother was creating life-endangering illnesses in her eight-year-old daughter by putting feces in her feeding tubes. Before these allegations were made public, the expense of the child's two hundred hospitalizations and forty surgeries moved her mother to seek publicity and donations. Her efforts paid off when she was invited to address the 1994 congressional hearings on Medicaid, and her daughter received a well-publicized visit from Hillary Clinton. This mother toured the country detailing the sacrifices she had made to provide proper medical care for her daughter and pleading for better insurance coverage to handle the exorbitant cost of hospitalizations and home care. The seriously ill daughter enabled this mother to gain attention and fame. A tip from suspicious medical staff members alleging Munchausen Syndrome by Proxy led to charges being brought against the mother, and the daughter was removed from her care. The life-threatening illnesses immediately stopped. The mother has recently begun championing the cause of parents "abused" by the social service system that takes their children away from them. Parents like this mother have a psychological disorder that compels them to use the health and well-being of their children to satisfy their own emotional needs.

I believe it is a similar need for personal gain (whether that need is conscious or unconscious) that drives the ABPD that pushes parents of high achievers to risk their children's physical and emotional health. Children and adolescents are routinely placed in dangerous situations for the purpose of a "higher goal," such as Olympic or professional sports, college scholarships, fame, or artistic accomplishment, with little or no consideration of the potential negative consequences to the child. All eyes are on the end result—not the process. ABPD is often difficult to pinpoint in the family relations of high-achieving children, but it is not rare or unique like Munchausen's. As parents we all are at risk for the self-serving rationalizations, projections, and delusions that form the core of ABPD.

For typical examples of ABPD, look around at almost any youth event. It is not at all unusual to find

A Billy who has been home with the flu for three days, pulled from his sick bed to "be tough" and play ball for the sake of his team

A Michelle who is competing bravely in a swim meet despite a broken bone in her foot

A Louise whose parents insist she practice her musical instrument several hours a day even when that means missing out on important school and social functions

You won't have to look far to find a child who is pushed onto the stage or into a competitive arena where she does not want to be. And certainly there are thousands of young children who are unhappily involved in activities, programs, and competitive events solely because their parents have been frustrated, thwarted, or disappointed in their own lives and need to regain a feeling of successful equilibrium through their children's accomplishments.

In serious situations, some parents risk their children's health and well-being by abusing their authority to dominate simply because they themselves are narcissistic, egomaniacal, greedy, or autocratic. There are stage mothers who angrily scold or even punish their children when they "blow" an audition. There are parents who impose severe emotional or physical consequences when their children earn anything less than a perfect test grade, and fail even to faintly praise the perfect score. There are those parents who coldbloodedly use their children's talents to pay the bills despite the dismantling of childhood this requires. And there are the infamous, caricatured sports parents who stand on the sidelines screaming, cursing, ridiculing, and demeaning every wrong move their young athlete makes. These parents rejoice in the errors of their child's opponents and abuse even teen referees with abandon. These parents risk the physical, emotional, and mental health of their children (and other's) in order to satisfy their own needs. They live in the world of Achievement by Proxy Distortion.

From Benign to Abusive

As you begin to examine the way you parent your high-achieving child, there are three stages of ABPD with which you should be familiar. The first sits precariously just beyond the edge of the normal range of behavior; the other two lie in the potentially problematic, even pathogenic and abusive range. Generally, ABPD behavior progresses slowly from fairly benign to potentially abusive. The next sections describe these three stages.

Risky Sacrifice

Risky sacrifice represents the mild loss of adults' ability to differentiate their own needs for success and achievement from a child's developmental needs and goals. At this level, adults apply increasing pressure (of a subtle but fairly easily comprehended nature) on a child to be a high achiever. Parents make real sacrifices, such as taking on a second or even a third job to support a child's pursuits. Families may move great distances, uprooting their entire household, in order to be closer to a gym or training facility; parents may allow a child to live at a training facility, and may even allow the child to be adopted into the custody of a coach or instructor. A parent may change jobs to have more time to dedicate to the child. A parent may even quit his own job and devote himself full time to his child's career as manager or coach or both. These decisions are often made with the best interest of the child at heart. But they are risky sacrifices that are often the first steps on a slippery slope to greater degrees of ABPD.

Once the family makes these kinds of major sacrifices, the child is expected to reciprocate with sacrifices of her own. She may be expected to maintain a certain weight. She may be required to practice tennis or golf eight hours a day. The child's social life with peers may be prohibited or indefinitely delayed in order to focus on a training regimen. These sacrifices are a form of repayment for the family sacrifice. The parent will say (or imply), "If I'm going to pay out all this money and arrange my life around your schedule, I expect you to do whatever you have to do—and more—to be the best." A deal has been struck. (See Step Four in Part Two for more information about risky sacrifices.)

Parents are not the only ones who can propose risky sacrifices to the high-achieving child. Marcy's dance instructor, for example, lectures her classes on the importance of weight control. She warns her students that successful dancers do not have time for dating and cannot even consider marriage or children until they are thirty years old. She does not demand a specific diet or require a no-date policy; she simply outlines the sacrifices that "successful" dancers accept. This instructor proudly insists to parents that she never puts any of her girls on a strict diet and would never interfere with their social development. But deep down she knows—and the dedicated, ambitious parents are aware—that she has planted and nurtured the seeds that grow into eating disorders and other life-endangering psychiatric disorders.

These implied expectations may push fourteen-year-old Marcy to adopt risky behaviors, or they may not. That's why this first step teeters on the edge between normal ABP and ABPD. That is why the ever-present potential for risky sacrifices frequently causes tension between parents and coaches or instructors. In this early stage of ABPD, reestablishing normal parental autonomy—for example, by parents' insisting that a child miss practice to participate in a school function—may produce unpleasant, even frightening situations in which an awe-inspiring, charismatic coach or instructor threatens to drop the child: "I guess there are others who are truly serious and may be more worthy of my valuable and limited time." For parents to resist this pressure requires both wisdom and courage. If the responsible adults cannot resist, they risk moving to the second level of ABPD: objectification.

Objectification

Objectification signals the loss of the adults' ability to differentiate their own needs and goals for success and achievement from those of the child. At this stage, the adults put increased pressure on the child, and she becomes increasingly defined by one activity in which she is able to perform well, adopting what has been called a unidimensional identity. This focus increasingly isolates the child socially, and potentially compromises her multiple developmental possibilities within the social, physical, and emotional spheres. The inability of adult caretakers to distinguish their own needs and goals from those of the child leads to their rationalizing of routine risk taking.

Rationalizations, which may be emotionally compelling, become major conscious and unconscious defensive strategies at this stage. Parents may adopt a helpless or even passive stance. Marcy's parents will insist, "I want my child to eat more and to train less, but if she insists on watching what she eats and on training eight hours a day, six days a week, how can I say no? I love my child." At the same time, the parents will show Marcy dieting tips, vaguely suggest that she is looking "a little chubby still," and express pleasure when she loses weight. Marcy will soon buy into this strategy and accept with relish a type of pseudoautonomy. "It is *my* decision to diet and to spend all my time practicing," she will say. "No one forces me to." Thus, when the child becomes ill, neither the parents nor the coach need feel responsible. Soon the parental obligation to protect the child's safety is diminished, and the amount of sacrifice demanded from the child comes to surpass defensible safe levels.

When a child has been objectified, parents, coaches, instructors, and sometimes entire media and government systems turn a blind eye to, if not passively and actively encourage and support, pathogenic behaviors. Once this happens, it is much more difficult for the adults to empathize with adolescent pain or experience. Emerging young, talented, and malleable entertainers, actors, musicians, and sports stars may distance themselves emotionally from their own feelings and collude in their own objectification in a process not dissimilar to Anna Freud's concept of identifying with the aggressor. A good example is the fourteen-year-old gymnast who, with the full knowledge of coach and parents, assumes full responsibility for training with a broken wrist. The child prodigy's body and mind become, even to the child, vessels to be driven and exploited in the pursuit of a "worthy" goal. "She can leave at any time" is a frequently heard statement from parents and coaches. The objectified child becomes the means to achieve an end, and that end justifies any and every conceivable means. (The topic of objectification will be further explored in Step Three.)

Abuse

Potentially abusive situations result from severe or complete loss of the adults' ability to differentiate their own needs and goals for success and achievement from those of the child. At this level, the child is at risk of becoming an objectified and exploited instrument of the adults' goals. These goals are pursued with little regard for short- and long-term physical and emotional morbidity or even mortality. By using powerful rationalizations, adults collude—often with the child—in perpetuating a process that is potentially life endangering, from both a psychological and physical standpoint.

As an example, at this level of ABPD Marcy's weight drops ten pounds, then another ten, and then another. Her parents and her instructor encourage her to eat more, but no one makes a committed move to take the situation seriously, because Marcy "looks good" and her performances remain excellent. During a dance performance, Marcy collapses on stage and is brought to the local hospital, where her parents are warned that she shows signs of malnourishment and a low potassium count, which could have fatal consequences if she develops a heart arrhythmia. It is recommended that she be evaluated for eating disorders and be admitted to a program. Upon physical recovery, Marcy insists she feels fine and is able to perform. She blames her collapse on fatigue and promises to rest more in the future. Eager to avoid blame and to avoid interrupting Marcy's training with medical and psychological evaluations, everyone lets Marcy make the decision to ignore the signs and symptoms of a severe problem. This is a life-endangering situation with neglectful and abusive overtones.

In these potentially abusive situations, the child has become the means to an end (such as establishing financial security, rebuilding the parent's lost sense of accomplishment or self-esteem, or building the coach or instructor's career). At this point it will be more difficult for the involved adults to empathize with the child. The youngster and adults may collude to have the youngster continue to compete despite frequent physical or emotional problems. The media and advertisers and the spectators they entertain and solicit may similarly endorse or glorify a potentially abusive interactive process. The risk to young participants is rationalized in favor of a vicarious sense of achievement, excitement, or glory. (See Step Six for the signs and symptoms of abuse.)

Healthy, Successful, and Sane

At the start it is difficult to identify when we cross over the line from normal ABP to abnormal ABPD because the roots of both grow from feelings and needs that are perfectly normal. Our children's accomplishments give us renewed enthusiasm for the possibilities in life. After all, with all that is gained it's true that the birth of a child initially involves loss: the loss of our own unlimited potential, the loss of freedom, the loss of the potential to realize all our ambitions. These are replaced with the realistic need to provide for a child to whom we may now transfer some of those lost dreams and goals. It is normal to say that children are extensions of ourselves—but only to a critical, well-defined point.

Once a child's exceptional talents begin to gain public attention, it becomes more of a challenge to separate our own and even the public's needs from the child's needs; this is when ABPD becomes more common. At this point, it is easy for parents to adopt a pseudo-passive stance, or rationalization. Parents may feel that their child's career and fame are like a runaway train, somehow out of their control. But while the child remains in their custody, nothing is further from the truth. Parents need not make a Faustian bargain, signing over critical parental responsibilities in exchange for success. Instead they need to be aware of the signs and symptoms of ABPD and strive to raise their children as unique individuals valued for their total person—not just their particular talent.

Through the seven-step program we detail in Part Two, you will be given the information you need to identify normal ABP behavior and abnormal ABPD. This information will help you ensure that your high-achieving children will reach their full potential yet will remain healthy, successful, and sane in their life and relationships.

PART II

A Seven-Step Program for Encouraging and Protecting High-Achieving Children

Step One

Evaluate "Talent"

Raising a child to reach his full potential can be difficult. Raising a high-achieving child can be especially challenging. As you will see in later chapters (or as you may already know), the talented child and his family often make many sacrifices in time, money, and commitment. So when your son or daughter starts participating or competing at a high level or starts dreaming about continuing an activity in college or even professionally, then it's time to evaluate if your child has the physical, emotional, and mental traits that are required of those who are successful in that field.

Can your child hold her own above the crowd? Are his talent and achievements exceptional? Does your child have the temperament, personality, commitment, and perseverance necessary to compete with the best? Will her talent stand the test of time? Are you feeding a dream that in the harsh light of reality will never be fulfilled against the quality competition? It's not pretentious or extreme to get answers to these questions—it's just commonsense parenting!

This chapter explains why you should objectively evaluate a child's talent in order to set realistic goals and why false and impractical goals and expectations can lead to Achievement by Proxy Distortion (ABPD). It discusses six factors that influence the evaluation of a child's talent: (1) skill level and ability, (2) age, (3) population and geographical base, (4) genetics, (5) personality and temperament, and (6) motivation for the short and long terms. The chapter also shares recommendations offered by those who professionally evaluate talent in the fields of athletics, academics, and the performing arts.

Why Evaluate Talent?

By definition, high-achieving children are considered elite only in terms of how they compare to other children. That's what makes them high achievers rather than low or average achievers. To advance to the top level of performance, your child will have to surpass the accomplishments of other highly talented children. Misjudging your child's talent level and forcing him to compete on a level that is not in synch with his natural capabilities can adversely affect his normal development. Similarly, a child with all the natural abilities in the world but without emotional and psychological resilience or balanced family support may also suffer greatly. Even if such a child achieves success, it may come at great physical and/or emotional cost.

The Perils of Overexpectation

Take the case of young Clara Woods. Her mother owned and operated a local dance studio. Since she was able to walk, Clara had the opportunity to study dance every day. Her mother wanted her daughter to dance professionally and live in the spotlight that had eluded her in her own life. Clara knew no other existence; she lived to dance. However, as Clara matured physically through early puberty, her body type came to resemble her father's: large, lumbering, and a bit uncoordinated. Clara's mother was so consumed by her visions of stardom for the both of them that she could not see the heartache ahead. She continued to insist that Clara lace up her ballet shoes and dance. Rather than exploring a range of talents and interests that might have better fit Clara's natural aptitudes, the thirteen-year-old was forced into situations that caused her embarrassment and humiliation in front of her peers. And all for the sole purpose of keeping her mother's dream alive!

This same overestimation of potential was the cause of family battles for the Miscuros. Young James was a standout baseball player in his small town. The youth league coaches told his father that James was the best they had ever seen and that they felt he had real potential to make it to the big leagues. James's whole identity became wrapped up in being a ball player. All his free time was spent practicing baseball, watching baseball on TV, reading about baseball, and dreaming about his future fame. At age fourteen, James was enrolled in a private high school with a reputation for winning state championships. It promised a very competitive baseball experience and frequent exposure to college recruiters. James's ambitious parents believed that the $10,000 per year cost would be a good investment that would be returned many times over by the college scholarship they expected James to earn.

Unhappily, in the spring of his freshman year, James joined the baseball team (which had a no-cut policy for freshmen) but sat on the bench the entire season. Although James and his parents had thought he was the next Cal Ripken Jr., on a larger scale, competing with boys from a wide geographical area, James's star no longer shone with exceptional brightness. His parents were furious. They felt cheated out of thousands of wasted dollars, for which James was indirectly blamed. Much more damaging, however, was the feeling they all had that at the age of fourteen, James was a failure in life.

The Value of Early Evaluation

In cases like those of Clara and James, an earlier objective evaluation could have helped the parents guide their children toward paths

ABPD Around the World

The Japanese way of education often means unrelenting pressure on families, biting competition between children, and fiery jealousy among parents. A critical spotlight has recently been cast on the lives of urban Japanese housewives, many of whom are cut off from extended families and left by work-obsessed husbands to raise children on their own. Critics say that with almost no life outside their homes, these women—called education mamas—measure their own self-worth by the academic achievements of their children (Coleman, 1999).

with more opportunities for self-fulfillment and success. Similarly, it could have helped inoculate the families against the bitter blow to pride and self-esteem they would experience should they continue undaunted with their dream.

Objective evaluation of a child's talent also helps parents avoid the ABPD pitfall of creating a pseudoprodigy—taking a perfectly healthy, normal, wonderful, but absolutely average child and putting him on the fast track to the top with nothing more than an inflated self-image. This happens quite often today because our society has put much emphasis on the value of giving children a strong sense of self-esteem. To achieve this we frequently praise the intent over the outcome or the process. It doesn't matter if Johnny can't read in the fifth grade; at least he's trying, and if I tell him he *can* read, then by George he can! It's not Jake's fault if he strikes out at a baseball game; it's the coach's fault. There are even schools that have removed the grading system so children never feel the sting of poor performance and inferior grades. All of this is well intentioned, but it also seeds long-term problems.

In the real world we live in, the fact is that some people do perform better than others. Some are more talented than others. Some deserve and get special recognition over others. All people are not equal in their abilities and achievements. If we insist that our very average children can be the best in anything they choose, we set them up for shame and failure. Not every female has what it takes to be a prima ballerina. Not every male has the physical attributes necessary to be a professional athlete. Not every child will have the intelligence to be class valedictorian. Not every child with mechanical ability will become a neurosurgeon. That's the reality of life, something both children and parents must accept, however grudgingly, even in an America where we like to think that any dream can come true.

The Labeling of All Kids as "Above Average"

This trend of labeling all children as special in all areas (even when they're not) has been called the Lake Wobegon Effect after humorist Garrison Keillor's description of the imaginary town of Lake Wobegon, where "all the children are above average." When physician John B. Cannel studied the Lake Wobegon Effect, he found that of the fifty state education departments, forty-nine reported above-average performance for their students (Elkind, 1989). Logic tells us that not all students can be above average if no one is average.

When average children are told they are "gifted," the stage is set for potential failure. For example, fourteen-year-old Chad Wakefield had been taking guitar lessons for five years. His parents gave him much encouragement and praise. Not wanting to dampen his enthusiasm or self-esteem, they listened without a word of criticism to performances that were always riddled with mistakes. They wanted him to feel good about his talent and himself. They didn't want to spoil the fun by focusing on technique or by insisting on consistent practice time. They assured Chad that he was a wonderful musician who would one day make his own records and become a star. Chad grew up believing he was a talented musician because his parents told him so and because in his small hometown there was no one to whom he could compare himself. He hit the wall when he tried to gain entrance into a select music college on the East Coast. He did not have the skill, the training, or the work ethic required of high-level musical performers. His inflated sense of his musical ability was not enough to carry him to a successful musical career.

In a similar way, certain gifted-and-talented school programs can set children up for a fall. There are no federal mandates or guidelines for defining giftedness or for creating specialized curriculum for these children. Each state is free to develop and implement its own program, and many states leave the details and the administration of these programs to each individual school district. Naturally, therefore, the term *gifted child* can mean many things to many people. It often happens that a school system will decide that a certain percentage of students from each grade level can be admitted into their program for gifted children. This keeps the enrollment steady and consistent from year to year.

But what if there are not that many truly gifted students in a particular grade level? In such a situation, many average children with good classroom grades and a teacher's recommendation are often accepted into the program and labeled gifted. This label can easily distort the way the child's family perceives her abilities and potential. Suddenly their gifted child is enrolled in Saturday morning rocket science classes. There is less time for play and more time devoted to compulsory study. As high school approaches, the child is scheduled for advanced placement classes and will struggle through night classes to prepare for standardized college entrance exams. Education becomes overly stressful, and the gifted student (who still remains quite average) is now called lazy when the grades begin to drop and the mismatch between expectation and real ability becomes apparent.

Of course there is nothing wrong with setting challenging educational standards and goals for all children. But labeling an average child as gifted can have unintended negative consequences in the same way that labeling that same child as learning disabled might. It can place her in an environment with a curriculum unsuited to her needs and abilities. But the opportunity to be called gifted, whether valid or not, is just too tempting a magnet for most parents to pass up.

Six Points of Talent Evaluation

The encouraging words "You can be anything you want to be in life" should be used with much caution. The U.S. Army's "Be all that you can be" slogan suggests a more realistic optimizing of real rather than imagined ability. Before you label your child as high achieving and put him on track for specialized training, you should realistically evaluate talent. To do this, consider the following six points.

Deadly Competition

When children compete for a spot on an athletic team, many parents bite their fingernails hoping for the best. But Texas mom Wanda Holloway decided to take action to ensure her thirteen-year-old daughter a spot on the cheerleading squad. The so-called cheerleader mom was convicted in 1991 of trying to hire a hit man to kill the mother of her daughter's cheerleading rival. Ms. Holloway said she wanted the mother killed because she believed that the daughter would be so upset that she would drop out of the competition. Witnesses at the trial described Holloway as a vindictive mother who was overzealous in pursuing her daughter's dreams.

Ability or Skill Level

Some high-achieving children are truly exceptional. They stand out from a very early age because their achievements far exceed developmental expectations. These children are the prodigies, the geniuses, the "blue chips." Their talent is affirmed by their instructors, their schoolteachers, and through various forms of testing. They are among the approximately 5 percent of the student population who are correctly labeled as gifted. In these cases, the exceptional talents of these children become evident at an early age to everyone around them—there is no doubt about their potential ability.

There is another 20 to 30 percent of the student population in the above-average range, where it is much tougher to determine what is truly high-level talent and what is not. In these cases, it is wise to have your child's skill or talent objectively evaluated if you find you are investing an exceptional amount of your money and your child's time into the development of this special ability.

The most crucial decision in useful skill evaluation is in the selection of the evaluator. As a parent, you should be automatically disqualified. Even if you are a professional dancer, you can not objectively evaluate the potential of your own child. Nature makes a parent's heart loving—and biased (and, even if unintentionally, potentially exploitative!). A child's team coach or classroom teacher or personal instructor may have interesting and helpful insights you should listen to, but they too usually cannot be fully objective and may not be trained to correctly evaluate exceptional ability.

Our advice is to arrange an evaluation with someone who is an expert in the field and has no potential to gain from the outcome. Personal gain would be a factor if, for example, the teacher of the local music school declared a child gifted and then recommended lessons three times a week at her school. Gain would be a factor if an academic testing service were financially connected to an after-school program for gifted students. This would also be the case if the coach who evaluates young athletes also runs a skill clinic that you have to sign up for in order to get the evaluation. Instead, look for professionals with nothing to gain.

Let's suppose James Miscuros, the baseball player mentioned earlier, had had an objective skill evaluation before enrolling in a private high school. It is very likely that his family would have learned that James's basic skill level and aptitude for the game was not as well developed as the other players known to be on the private school's baseball team. The family might have been forewarned that there was a strong possibility that James would not be a starting player on a very competitive team. Armed with this information they might have decided to leave James in his local public school, where he would easily make the baseball team and have the opportunity to play in every game and improve his performance. From the $10,000 they saved, they might have invested a small amount in private lessons. After another year of both physical and skill development, James could have been evaluated again; the evaluation would have indicated that James was ready to transfer into the more competitive program—or that he was just not one of the top players in the area. Either way, James would be playing ball on the level most compatible with his skill and feeling good about himself. And his parents would not be angry about wasting time and money.

An objective skill evaluation should not be taken as an indisputable mandate of a child's potential. It is merely a way to objectively compare a child to the rest of the talented population and to gain insight into where she stands at that moment. A good skills evaluation will suggest areas of weakness that need more work; it will offer specific steps for improvement; it will outline both the weak and the strong. This information can help the family make decisions about future lessons, programs, and camps that are based on realistic expectations and goals. All of this saves a child from being thrown into a level that is higher or lower than her capabilities.

Age

Ideally, all children should be allowed to experiment for years with many different facets of their personality and abilities before they are labeled a high achiever in any one area. They should be given time to understand themselves and their world before one talent is identified and they are put on track to perfect it to the exclusion of all others. In the ideal world, children are given time to explore who they are and who they want to become.

But in our highly competitive, race-to-the-top world, parents often feel that they owe it to their children to get them on the right track early so they have an advantage over the throngs of other

A Little Fish in a Big Bowl

"It can be a big adjustment for the talented dancers who are accepted into the School of American Ballet. They've been such a big fish in their local pond at home that it's easy to become discouraged when they find out that everybody here is a big fish. They've left home, given up their friends, and then find out that they're no longer 'the best.' That's tough to adjust to. They also know that their parents have sacrificed a lot of time and money to get them to this point, and the local papers have probably written up a story about the local dancer going to study at a prestigious dance school in the big city. There's a lot of pressure on them to succeed, and some kids realize they just aren't cut out to do what it takes to get to the next level."

Peter Libman, director of student life,
School of American Ballet

"contenders." In evaluating a child's talent, a parent has the often difficult task of determining when intensive training at an early age is absolutely necessary and, very important, when it is not.

Let's look first at very young children. Love and admiration for a child's talents and abilities aside, if your child is under age ten, be honest and practical in your evaluation. Most precocious children are just that: out of the gate faster than others, but not really more gifted over time. In the vast majority of cases, it is not necessary to put these children on a specialized fast track that excludes the development of other areas of talent and interest. In the area of academics, for example, the ability to grasp complex concepts develops at different rates in different children. Some may excel early at reading or math; others may instead focus on their social or physical skill development first and then turn their attention to their cognitive development when they are ready. Gradually, these children's skills plateau on equal ground. This is sometimes upsetting news for parents who are sure their little Zachary is a genius because he is so much smarter at age four than his classmates. Zachary may indeed be academically gifted, but it is just too early to say for sure. This is an iffy time to evaluate and label almost any area of talent. This should come as good news for parents who worry that their preschooler is "slow" in comparison to children like Zachary. Young children need opportunities and experiences and encouragement to blossom fully in all areas—and, most important, they need time. *The Einstein Papers* reveal the elementary school teacher who insisted nothing good could possibly be expected of young Albert. Thank goodness there isn't a cutoff date for determining the academic talent of a human being.

Athletics is another area where the evaluation of talent must consider the age of the child. In youth league sports of every type, it is very common to find kids who are unbeatable: the little leaguer who hits home runs every time up at bat, the soccer star who can't be stopped as she flies past the defense and scores the hat trick, the pee-wee football star who is the team's touchdown hero. A casual observer may say, "This kid's got talent. You should get him on select teams and start competing on a higher level. You've got a gold mine here." What you probably have here is a kid who is physically bigger and stronger than the others. These young athletes excel thanks to their early maturation and to such factors as speed, coordination, and strength. Shane Murphy, a sports psychologist and the former president of the Division of Exercise and Sport Psychology of the American Psychological Association, tells us in his book *The Cheers and the Tears* (1999, p. 77) that reliance on these talents often diminishes the attention the young stars pay to skill development and technique, which comes back to hurt them as they grow older and encounter more competition. He says that studies indicate that very few kids who are the big stars on their youth teams ever end up being successful in professional or Olympic sports. It's our observation that when the other kids grow to match their muscle or level of coordination (often at puberty), these early standouts frequently drop out. Unfortunately, their self-image had become wrapped up in the "star" label, and they can't adjust to being "just" a team player.

The race to the top does begin very early in some athletic arenas, however, and those who miss the early jump may very well never be able to get on track for high-level achievement. Like it or not, age can become a definite consideration when judging talent in areas that require specialized large-muscle training and early competitive performance. Such activities as gymnastics, figure skating, and dancing, for example, sometimes require intensive training for young children. Consider figure skating. If a fourteen-year-old girl goes to a skating coach and says she would like to begin lessons so she can perform in the Olympics, the astute coach will more than likely encourage the girl to take up the sport for other, less competitive reasons. She can learn the skills of skating for personal growth and enjoyment, but the possibility of starting so late and making it to the Olympics is very, very hard-to-even-imagine slim.

In most fields, there are no hard-and-fast rules about when a child should get on the specialized, high-intensity training track, but we asked around to find out what the experts think. Here is what we found:

- *Is it necessary for a serious musician to begin focused lessons at a young age?* It depends. We could find no one at the renowned Juilliard School in New York City who felt that formal musical instruction before the age of ten was a prerequisite to future success. Andrew Thomas, Juilliard's director of precollege admissions, noted that piano and string players often begin training before age ten, but that's simply because they are physically able to do so, not because it is necessary to later success. Brass and woodwind players can't start early, he reminds us, because they don't have the required lung capacity.

The age of thirteen, however, becomes a magical cutoff date for some musicians. In his book *Why Michael Couldn't Hit*, Harold Klawans (1998) explores studies that have been done on the brains of young violinists. Becoming an accomplished violinist requires the brain to give rapid and complex directions to the fingers of both hands in response to visual or aural clues. Magnetic resonance imaging (MRI) shows evidence that a violin virtuoso has to start playing before the age of thirteen. Not fourteen, not fifteen, but before the age of thirteen. The MRIs of those who had started at age three or four looked no different than those who started at eleven or twelve. The abrupt change occurred between the ages of twelve and thirteen. Those who hadn't started by thirteen never caught up. The circuits they activated were smaller, less complex, and more restricted. The time frame during which their brains could be guided to select those circuits had come and gone and left them forever without that ability. The findings of this research may be generalized to other highly complex motor skills. Klawans wonders if these studies can explain why Michael Jordan, despite his wonderful, if not incomparable, athletic skills, as an adult couldn't learn to hit a baseball.

- *Can a twelve-year-old girl begin gymnastic lessons in the hopes of earning Olympic gold?* Probably not. A gymnastics coach who owns a very competitive school for young girls tells us that it will depend on the level at which the child begins and how quickly she can advance through the upper levels. Levels one through three are usually in-house learning programs that are not competitive. You'll usually see the really talented eight-year-olds and younger being fast-tracked up to level four and five. Twelve-year-olds who are still on level four or five are called plumbers in the business: they're the kids who don't have quite the same physical ability. They have heart and they work hard, but the other kids have left them in the dust. The administration of the system forces the talented kids through quickly so they can reach the high levels at a young age and be competitive in a system that focuses on young girls. It would be tough for a twelve-year-old to come in cold and make it to the top, but not impossible. (Note: the Olympic committee has just recently changed the age requirement for gymnasts. Athletes must be at least sixteen years old to compete. This change is intended to give girls more time to grow and develop before they are put into such a high-pressure situation.)

- *Must a bright student get on the fast track to an Ivy League school by attending a notable and prestigious preschool?* No. The present dean of admissions at Princeton University candidly admitted to us, "I am unaware of any evidence to suggest that attending preschool, let alone a particular preschool, has any effect, one way or the other, on a child's later chances for admission at an Ivy League school. No college I am familiar with even inquires about an applicant's grammar school education, let alone any preschool an applicant may have attended."

- *Must a naturally talented young performer sign with a talent agent and audition for children's parts to get to know (and be known) in the right circles if she wants to be a star?* Not necessarily. Although none of the many Broadway actors we have interviewed consider early experience in the theater a necessary step to a theatrical career, it clearly is an advantage in the TV and movie world, where several careers are possible in a lifetime.

Parenting takes patience. It's tempting to rush the high-achieving young scholar, athlete, or performing artist into an intensive training regimen, but it's best to get a professional opinion about the need for an early start—and as we said before, choose that professional wisely. Don't ask your child's instructor for this advice; his or her income depends on young children dedicating themselves early. Do as we did: call a nearby school or instructor who has no ties to your child and ask for an objective expert opinion.

Population Base and Geographical Area

Sometimes children appear to excel because they are far superior in talent to others in their school or town (or both). These children are often put on an accelerated track, and their families make many financial and personal sacrifices to encourage the child's continued success. It can happen, however, that the child excels only in comparison to others in his close environment, not to others in his field—the small fish in the small pond syndrome. Let's say, for example, that a boy is the best golfer his small Midwestern town has ever seen. However, if he should ever go on the junior tour with children from Las Vegas or from states like North Carolina, where kids are raised with a golf club in their hands, he'll find that his skill is not really competitive. He becomes the small fish in the ocean who gets gobbled up by the sharks.

The same can happen to any performing artist who might stand out as a rising star in a small, rural community, but who might look quite average at a national event that brings in children from many large city areas. This happens also to children mislabeled as academically gifted by their school programs. In these cases, parents are willingly misled into thinking that their children are more intelligent and can achieve more academically than they are in fact capable of. This becomes apparent when these children attend a high school or college with other truly gifted students.

When talented youngsters compete on a national level or for college scholarships, they compete with the best from all over the country. Parents who are sure that their child is the best and who therefore invest a great deal of time and money in her training should consider how she compares on a national level if they have expectations that their child will reach the top.

A parent struggling with ABPD will be blind to the possibility that the child's talent is exaggerated by her small environment. Then when reality hits (as in the case mentioned earlier of James Miscuros, the baseball player who enrolled in a private school for the opportunity to play on their competitive team but then didn't get the opportunity to get off the bench), the parents become angry about the "wasted" money and effort, and the child feels like a failure.

Getting an objective skill evaluation that considers the child's level of ability compared to the broader world is one way to factor in the population and location influence. You can also better evaluate your child's talent by competing in events out of your area; attending regional and state events, even as spectators; watching televised competitions; and by joining regional, state, or national organizations that distribute information in your child's field of accomplishment.

Genetics

We all want to encourage our children to reach for the stars. We want them to believe the world is theirs for the asking. But we must eventually temper this message with the reality that some vocations, some accomplishments, require certain inborn traits, characteristics, abilities, and physical attributes. Because of the cards they've been dealt at birth, not all people can become professional athletes. Not everyone can go to Ivy League schools or join Mensa. Not everyone is able to sing with the Metropolitan Opera Company. This sounds discriminatory—and it is, as far as it's discriminatory to keep most short people off competitive basketball teams or to keep shy, introverted people off the Broadway stage. Sometimes a person's biological makeup has to match his desire for achievement.

It is well known that in some instances there must be a genetic physical suitability to the talent. An overweight or large-sized female teen is unlikely to have a successful career as a ballerina, gymnast, or diver. In the same way, a small and frail male teen is fighting the odds if he wants a football or basketball scholarship to an NCAA

Division I school. This is a fact that parents and their young athletes have to consider before sacrificing their time, money, and selves to this pursuit.

Let's say, for example, that little John wants to sing in Broadway musicals. When he is very young, this goal amuses his parents, who encourage him to be in school plays. Soon they are investing a great deal of time and money in voice and acting lessons, in community theater productions, and in trips to New York to see professional plays. But as John reaches middle childhood, it is glaringly apparent that he is tone deaf: he cannot sing on pitch. His voice teacher cautions John's parents that John will not win auditions for serious musical productions. Here is where John's parents can choose between two roads: one that will support the child's progress and development, the other that can distort them.

To support John the person (who is not one and the same as John the singer), they can tell their son the truth and guide him to dramatic roles where he can stay involved in theater of another kind. Or they might encourage him to study a musical instrument so that he can remain involved in the musical theater environment. Or they can introduce him to stage directing or production. They can also encourage him to continue singing his heart out for his own enjoyment.

On the other road, if John's parents are at risk for ABPD, they may put their own needs ahead of their son's. They might blame the problem on the voice instructor's incompetence. They could drag John from one teacher to another, from one production to another, intent on finding someone who will recognize their son's true talent. They may continue to blame his persistent failure in this field on other people and circumstances. They may turn their disappointment into determination, instituting a grueling training schedule to overcome this "little problem." When this approach doesn't work, they will angrily blame their son for not trying hard enough. In reality, if blame must be laid somewhere, it should be set at the feet of the parents, who pass on inherited traits.

To evaluate a child's in-born traits and characteristics, many parents turn to professionals. They may have a promising young musician's pitch tested at the music department of a local university. They may have the IQ of a budding scholar professionally tested. Parents can have a young athlete's bones x-rayed to estimate how tall he will grow. Some will have a neurological exam to evaluate coordination and gross- or fine-motor skill development.

Professional evaluation of genetic traits and potential is not a new or far-fetched idea. Tennis coach Boris Breskvar, who trained champions like Steffi Graf and Boris Becker, always required detailed physiological measurements to allow, among other things, accurate prediction of ultimate growth. Boris Becker, for example, was expected to grow to six-foot-three. (His adult height is six-foot-three and one centimeter.) This early finding made it worthwhile for his training to concentrate on the serve-and-volley game, whereas if he were expected to be a shorter player, a baseline game would have been better (Radford, 1990).

If your child's future depends on certain genetic programming and you want to know now what's in the cards, a trained professional may be able to help.

Personality and Temperament

Success on an elite level is more probable if an individual has certain personality traits. The traits you can evaluate in your child are his mental toughness, level of optimism, trainability, and work ethic. These qualities are helpful to building the emotional stamina often needed in highly competitive arenas.

Mental Toughness

Mental toughness or resiliency is the ability to persist through difficult times, to stay determined when things aren't going smoothly, to get back up after a fall. A simple way to test one aspect of mental toughness is to watch the way your child responds to criticism. On the road to the top, some kids can't deal with it at all and drop out, and others can handle anything you throw at them and keep going. This trait comes naturally to some and can be learned by others through a combination of balanced reinforcement strategies that deal with both positive and negative events. These strategies teach children that *effort* is important and that a negative event is a single occurrence and not a defining outcome. A child can be encouraged to try again at a lower level and then increase the level slowly. Adults can model resiliency skills by showing children through example how they can still get back on the horse after a fall. By always allowing a child many roads to or opportunities for success, parents can reinforce the idea that failure to attain a positive outcome despite strong, honest effort in one area provides learning opportunities for future success. Mental toughness is not only valuable for reaching the top in a certain area; it's a valuable life skill no matter where your children land.

Level of Optimism

The majority of successful high achievers have a solid can-do attitude. They look at defeat as an opportunity to learn something and do it right the next time. (It was Edison who is often quoted as saying after yet another unsuccessful attempt, "I've just learned 473 ways not to build a light bulb.") They don't let a setback demoralize them. They are willing to take risks to get to the next level and to reach their potential. Watch how your child faces a simple challenge: Does she look to you to solve it for her? Does she give up too quickly? Does she admit defeat without a fight? If she does, she needs some training in positive thinking if she wants to compete with the big guys. If you know your child is exceptionally talented, don't let her walk away from a problem muttering "I'm no good," "I can't do it," or "I'll never be better than the other kids." Take a look at Martin Seligman's book *The Optimistic Child* (1996) for some great tips on how to encourage a positive attitude.

Trainability

High-achieving children are often naturally gifted in their area of strength, but almost all need guidance, instruction, and coaching to reach their full potential. To work intensely with someone and get the most benefit from the lesson, a child needs to be what some people call trainable or coachable. This trait entails a willingness to be molded in a certain direction by a trained instructor. The child must be obedient and willing to listen. This does not mean that the child should do whatever he is told like a robot, without thinking of the consequences. But it does mean that the instructor is in charge during the lesson. Children who spend the majority of their lesson time arguing with their instructor or coach are demonstrating one of two things: (1) they really are smarter and better than their teacher and should be training with someone on a higher level, or (2) they have a resistant personality that will make it difficult for them to improve and compete against other high achievers on the top levels.

If you see that your child resists direction and instruction, you don't need to insist that he forfeit all independent thought and the right to question or challenge. But it does mean that he should learn how to evaluate instruction and how to challenge only when necessary.

Let's take a simple softball situation, for example: If a player is given the bunt sign with two outs and she disagrees, what should she do? Some kids will completely ignore the sign and do what they think is best. This obviously is a quick way to infuriate a coach and end up on the bench. Other kids will throw some version of a public tantrum by stepping out of the batter's box and arguing with the coach—another bad move that is not going to be good for the player. The smart, coachable player will call time out, privately explain her misgivings about that call, and then return to the plate and do exactly what the coach says is best. That's a kid who is trainable but also has a head on her shoulders.

Work Ethic

Everybody knows that it takes a lot of hard work to be a high achiever. But too many kids work continuously only on their strong points—the things that make them feel good. The kids with the most potential are the ones who can recognize that opportunity often comes disguised as drudgery. They are willing to work just as hard on their weak areas. If Carl is a standout basketball player because he has a strong jump shot, you'll see him on the practice courts working on his defense, not his jump shot. If Kate can hit a softball better than anyone on the team, she will spend much of her practice time working on her running speed and fielding. If Jenna can do her tap routine in her sleep but can't quite master her jazz number, that's where she'll put her efforts. If Craig whizzes through his math homework, he'll turn more time and attention to the English assignment that's giving him trouble. Although it's natural to want to do the things that come easy, a child's willingness to work on the things that are not so immediately rewarding will tell you a lot about the strength of her work ethic.

Motivation

David Feigley, sports psychologist and chair of the Department of Movement Science at Rutgers University, tells us that motivation can become more important than talent. He says, "There are people who have physically willed themselves to the top despite a skill evaluation that should have held them back." There's no doubt that a desire to succeed is certainly a driving force behind most people who reach the top in their fields. The question then is, Is your child motivated enough to push past the difficulties and the sacrifices that are required to be the best? Does your child have that inner spark? That fire? That passion?

Before you jump in to answer, remember this: motivation in a child is not the same as motivation in an adult. If your eight-year-old wants to play pro basketball, you may not see the kind of motivation that drives a high school senior to practice several hours a day and sacrifice other activities for the sport. You may not see a burning desire to attend programs that are boring, repetitious, or overly demanding. This doesn't mean your child isn't motivated; young children know there are just too many other things in the world to be interested in to sacrifice too much time and effort to one area. Don't misinterpret this scattering of interest as lack of motivation.

The most important motivation factor that can be evaluated in a child is the *source* of the child's initial desire to participate in the particular activity. To succeed past middle childhood, the child must be *self*-motivated; he must have an internal desire to excel. When evaluating your child's level of motivation, you should ask yourself whether he is externally or internally motivated. Does he excel to impress others? To earn a scholarship? To maintain a reputation? To please his parents? If he does, then he is externally motivated; soon the use of his skill will become a chore, and burnout becomes likely. But if he loves what he does, if he thinks it is fun, if he would want to continue even if his parents weren't there to push him, if he has the self-discipline to do what's necessary, then he is internally motivated and is likely to be successful in his field.

Of course it's natural to push and nudge your children a bit to guide them in the right direction. It's even natural to nag them to practice, and to insist on certain rules, such as early curfews before big events. But you must do these things knowing that at some stage of the child's development you must let go of your own hopes for your child and trust him to pursue his own goals—even if they aren't the ones you had nurtured. If a child is not self-motivated to begin with, he will not make it to the top once out of his parents' control.

A local high school baseball star in my town is a good example of what can happen when accomplishment is built on external motivation. This boy made his father very proud when he accepted an athletic scholarship to college but then quit the baseball team after the first season. The boy's father was devastated; he became deeply depressed and refused to even talk to his son for several years. This parent was obviously caught up in ABPD; his own life was defined by his boy's success in baseball. Although sad, this occurrence is not rare. This often happens when a young adult goes to college and no longer feels obliged to please everyone else. Is this person a failure? The parent may think, "I put all my hopes on this child, and he disappointed me." But for the kid, it isn't a failure at all; it's a triumph of letting go of other people's goals that were not his own.

It's wonderful to offer our children the opportunity to be the best, but that's not enough. Our children must be internally motivated to reach for the top. Ask yourself, If I stopped pushing my child, would she continue on this path on her own? The answer will tell you where her motivation is coming from.

A Gymnast's Growing Pains

At the age of seventeen, Olympic gymnast Dominique Moceanu filed for the right to be declared a legal adult. The lawsuit alleged that a trust fund in her name was being squandered by her father and that she had been deprived of a "regular" childhood. She told reporters, "I want to be able to train and compete in the sport I love for the right reason, because I love it, not because my father tells me I have to make more money."

ADVICE FROM THE EXPERTS

As we've seen, the best way to get an objective evaluation is to seek out people who evaluate talent for a living and find out where your child stands in comparison to others. We've asked three experts what they look for when evaluating exceptional talent. The experts are (1) Chuck Schnabel, director of Raising Confidence Skills Corporation, (2) Peter D. Rosenstein, executive director of the National Association for Gifted Children, and (3) Ellen Savitz, M.Ed., principal of the Philadelphia High School for Creative and Performing Arts.

Athletics

Chuck Schnabel is the director of Raising Confidence Skills Corporation, which counsels and evaluates athletes. He is also a professional baseball scout for the Philadelphia Phillies. Schnabel offers the following information about skill evaluation for athletes.

"An objective skill evaluation is absolutely necessary. For professional baseball we have specific criteria an athlete has to meet: you have to run the sixty-yard dash in x amount of seconds; catchers have to throw to second base in a specific time period; pitchers have to achieve x amount of miles per hour on certain pitches. Every sport has requirements, and kids need to know if they have the potential to rise to that mark. You can get this information by getting an objective skill evaluation—which can be difficult to get from your child's coach. You need to find somebody who knows the sport and has nothing personally or financially to gain from your child. I suggest trying showcases, camps, and clinics that evaluate players. [See Step Two.]

"Simple genetics also plays a role in athletic talent. We definitely look for certain physical profiles in athletes. For example, in baseball, if you're long, lean, and strong and make some mistakes, it's no big deal. But if you're short and stocky and make the same mistakes, your other skills better be very strong to overcome any shortcoming. Of course, kids still have a lot of growing to do, but let's say in a sport like basketball, if Mom and Dad are both short, there's not a strong chance that Junior will be getting a basketball scholarship when he finishes growing.

"Before parents put a lot of time and money (and high hopes) into an athletic program, they should take their young athletes for a thorough physical exam with an eye toward estimated growth and estimated natural weight. They should ask how much weight this child's skeleton and heart can stand. A sports-oriented physician can give you a real good look at what the future holds physically. Don't ask your child's coach for this information. Most know only what the team needs, not always what's best for each player. It's not unusual for a high school football coach to tell a kid who weighs 175 that he wants him to weigh 200 by next season or for a wrestling coach to ask for a difficult weight reduction. These expectations are a prescription for danger and if medically unsupervised, can lead to abuse of performance-enhancing drugs.

"Also important is a thorough eye exam. Ask the ophthalmologist to check depth perception and color perception. Many kids do not hit breaking pitches because they do not see them correctly. Subtle eye problems can affect a kid's performance in any sport.

"If an athlete has the skill and genetic build required to compete in her sport, then we'll take a closer look at what we call makeup. Makeup is the word we use to encompass personality, temperament, and trainability. I try to judge what kind of individual this person is. What are her goals? How badly does she want to do this? How well does she listen to instruction? These things all say a lot about a kid's potential to be a good athlete. I also want to know the source of the kid's motivation. Does the kid really want to play, or are the parents pushing her to play? This has a lot to do with the athlete's future potential, so I need to find this out right away. We look for parents who are knowledgeable, fair, and willing to accept reality. If they're looking for personal financial gain or public recognition, that's a bad sign.

"Another thing I look for is the burnout factor. It's possible to play your sport too much. Kids need some time to take a break. That's a problem with kids I've seen in states like Florida and California, where they play baseball all year round. They may be proficient sooner, but many of these kids just aren't as aggressive or as anxious to play as kids I see from the states where weather forces them to take a break. The kids who don't overplay have more fire, and that's an important trait to have if you want to play in college or in the pros."

Academics

Peter D. Rosenstein, executive director of the National Association for Gifted Children in Washington, D.C., reminds us that one of the only reasons to evaluate the academic abilities of a child in school is for proper placement in the educational system. He says that giftedness indicates a need, not a gold star.

You may notice behaviors or characteristics that indicate a need for testing. A representative of the ERIC Clearinghouse on Disabilities and Gifted Education directed us to the organization's website (http://ericec.org) for a list (supplied by the Council for Exceptional Children) of early traits typical of gifted children:

- Abstract reasoning and problem-solving skills
- Advanced progression through developmental milestones
- Early and extensive language development
- Early recognition of caretakers (for example, smiling)
- Enjoyment and speed of learning
- Excellent sense of humor
- Extraordinary memory
- High activity level
- Intense reactions to noise, pain, or frustration
- Less need for sleep in infancy
- Long attention span
- Sensitivity and compassion
- Perfectionism
- Unusual alertness in infancy
- Vivid imagination (for example, imaginary companions)

Your personal observations, your child's school achievement, input from the child's teachers, and results of standardized tests of intelligence can all help you decide if you would like your child to have an objective and professional evaluation of intelligence. To locate information on identification and screening procedures used by the school districts, a representative from the

Council for Exceptional Children recommends that you contact any or all of the following:

- The person responsible for gifted education in your state. A list is available on the following website: ericec.org/fact/stateres.htm.
- The state or local advocacy group. State groups are offered on the aforementioned website. You might find local advocacy groups by asking the state group or your child's school, or by searching citizen testimony before the school board.
- Local school district offices that are responsible for student assessment—for example, the counseling or student services department. Ask what tests and procedures are used to select students for programs for gifted students. (Also ask if the testing must be done by school personnel; schools do not have to, and often will not, recognize the results of out-of-district, private testing.)

Evaluation of gifted children often includes some type of standardized test. A fact sheet from the Council for Exceptional Children explains that these instruments can assess a wide variety of capabilities, aptitudes, or scholastic abilities—for example, abstract thinking skills, academic skills, artistic ability, creative thinking and creativity, general acquired knowledge, intellectual ability, leadership, motivation, nonverbal and verbal reasoning, and problem-solving ability.

Examples of specific tests include the Cognitive Abilities Test (COGAT), Gifted and Talented Evaluation Scales (GATES), the Iowa Tests of Basic Skills, Scales for Rating the Behavioral Characteristics of Superior Students, the Kaufman Assessment Battery for Children (K-ABC), and Raven's Progressive Matrices. Most of these tests are not considered IQ tests. Like all assessments, IQ tests vary in what they measure. However, IQ tests are usually given individually; those that are given individually are generally the most comprehensive and most reliable. The Wechsler Intelligence Scale for Children (WISC) and the Stanford-Binet are examples of individually administered tests. They are administered by a licensed psychologist or practitioner. Specific information on tests is located at the ERIC Clearinghouse on Assessment and Evaluation (http://ericae.net).

Performing Arts

Ellen Savitz, M.Ed., is the principal of the Philadelphia High School for Creative and Performing Arts. Her job is to identify and nurture young artists. We asked her what she looks for as a sign of potential talent in young performing artists.

"The display of talent at an audition is only the beginning of what it takes to be successful in this school and in the world of performing arts. Because we're a public school, we get over 3,000 applications for 170 spots each year. Some of these students have been taking lessons and practicing their talent for years, but other, often poorer, students haven't had that opportunity and yet still may show signs of raw ability. So we need to look for more than practiced talent.

"We look for passion and commitment. A student who loves what he's doing and is willing to put in a lot of time and hard work to improve has a much better chance of being successful in this field than an exceptionally talented and trained artist who is lazy or who has a "star" attitude. One of the things we look at before accepting a student is the attendance record. That tells us a lot about self-discipline and commitment. If you haven't been able to get yourself out of bed and into school in the past, you'll never make it in the arts. It takes so much hard work and unselfish dedication. Our kids work late into the night; they often give up their Saturdays and Sundays. They work hard until they get it right, all while carrying a full academic load.

"You can't stay in this school if you don't perform well in the classroom. Success in schoolwork is what gives students options whether they make it big as performing artists or not. I have said that our biggest "failure" is the popular performing group Boyz to Men, who graduated from here; they are in the small minority who did not go to college. But now that they have had years of traveling around the world and are getting older and tired of that kind of life, several of them have enrolled in college business classes so they can operate their own recording studio and continue in a performance-related field if they choose to stop playing and touring themselves. In our school, you can't even have the lead in a play if you aren't an exceptional student first.

"Once students are accepted and enrolled, we have more opportunity to judge the personality characteristics that are associated with success. We give them many opportunities for ensemble work because they need to learn that a star is only as good as the players around her. The ability to work as a member of a team—and not be the star—is very important. We also look for a degree of mental toughness. Being a performing artist is like taking your guts out, throwing them on the stage, and saying, "Here, walk all over my insides." It's not easy to put yourself out there knowing you might fail—you might meet with criticism. And there's no way you can do that if you don't love what you do. The motivation to pursue the arts has to come from inside the individual; no one else can push you forward.

"Parents can drag their young children to a hundred auditions all over the country if they're real stage parents, but once children reach high school age, you can't make them perform. They just won't do it with their heart, and that shows. If a parent pushes a child into this school, he won't last more than a year. It takes too much work and time to be successful in the performing arts to do it unless you really want it inside yourself.

"This dedication and commitment is what gives kids the advantage that's needed in this field. I remember when one of our students went to New York to audition for a dramatic role and learned this lesson. This girl was extremely beautiful and talented. She came back from New York with the realization that the world is full of extremely beautiful and talented girls. She saw firsthand that it would take more than that to make it.

"I believe that it takes more than pure talent to make it big in any field. The dedication, commitment, mental toughness, teamwork skills, and perseverance that our students show in their pursuit of perfection in the performing arts will assure them success in any role they may choose in life."

There is no magic formula for evaluating the talent of high-achieving children, nor is there an exact moment of opportunity to do so.

The physical, emotional, and mental traits required for success in a given field are varied and often elusive. But the child who expects to compete for a place among the top performers will eventually need to stand up and be evaluated in comparison to the thousands of other hopefuls. Getting an objective evaluation before your child is thrown out into the crowd will give you the information you need to make beneficial decisions and sacrifices for your child.

In Step Two, we will take a look at the classes, schools, camps, and programs that give exceptional children the opportunity to improve their skills, compare their abilities to other high-achieving children, and build a reputation by distinguishing themselves among the best.

Step Two

Selecting Classes, Schools, and Camps That Cater to High-Achieving Children

Once you have confirmed that your child has exceptional talent, you will find there is no limit to the ways that her talent can be nurtured, honed, and encouraged. There are highly specialized classes, schools, and camps in every part of the country that cater to any possible talent a child might have up his sleeve. For the young athlete there are elite, select, and traveling teams, camps, and showcases. For the academically inclined there are Saturday and after-school classes, and summer camps focusing on everything from rocketry to poetry. And for the budding performing artists there are schools and camps as well as group and individualized instruction with highly touted and credentialed artists.

As ambitious but also pragmatic parents, we want our high-achieving children to have these extras that we hope will give them an advantage in their quest to earn an acceptance or a scholarship to a good college, or to launch them toward a professional career. And so we scan the catalogues and surf the Web looking for the best classes, programs, instructors, camps, and schools. Sometimes these extra learning opportunities are around the corner and quite inexpensive. But often the very best programs are far away and extravagantly priced. Sometimes they are programs that are fun, instructional, and well worth the time and effort required to participate. Other times they are grueling, intense, and stressful. How can you find the one that's best for your child and your family?

This chapter will help you look where you're going before you jump onto the "extra advantage" bandwagon. It will help you evaluate your motives for signing your kids up for "more." And it will help all parents avoid the ABPD trap of sending their talented young people out willy-nilly all over the country grasping at some elusive and illusory gold ring of success without clearly knowing what they are likely to gain or lose in the process.

All our children can go to the free, local public school; they all have the opportunity to play on free and convenient school or recreational sport teams; and they can easily take inexpensive dance, music, or acting lessons at a local studio. But high achievers often outgrow the usefulness of programs created and geared for the general population. They need more of a challenge. They need more opportunities to improve their skills. They need a higher level of competition. They need more exposure to other children more like themselves. For these reasons, it often makes sense (at least on paper) to take our children out of the free local programs and place them where their needs are better met—in distant and expensive programs.

To minimize and, one hopes, prevent the influence of ABPD, I ask the families I work with to think carefully before placing their children in specialized programs. I ask them to think about the many inconveniences and emotional and financial costs that will be involved and then ask themselves the question, Why? Why is this environment important for *me* in the development of my child's potential? Knowing what results or accomplishments you expect from your child in any given situation will help you avoid throwing her into places where she can get hurt, worn out, overused, or exploited. It will also give you enough humility and wisdom to remove her from a program you see causing some of these problems.

There are many, many reasons why children are enrolled in specialized schools and programs. Some of these reasons are sound and healthy ones. Others are possibly exploitative and dangerous. Some offer a Faustian mixture of the two. Before you sign your child up for more of anything, consider these four possible motives for your decision:

1. Improvement of skills
2. Supportive environment
3. Elite exposure
4. Résumé building

Each of these is a reasonable motive, yet each has the potential for creating an ABPD situation. The following discussion will help you draw that line between nurturing and pushing your children.

Motive One: Improvement of Skills

High-achieving children generally have observable talent, but that talent alone is usually not enough to keep them out in front. The talent needs to be nurtured and guided in constructive directions.

Ten-year-old Donna, for example, is a real math whiz. However, her local public school is not able to individualize a program to meet her daunting talent, so her parents have enrolled her in a Saturday class at a local university that offers advanced instruction in mathematics for children her age. They have also hired a private tutor to help keep her advanced skills sharpened, and they are looking for a good summer camp that will challenge her abilities while simultaneously keeping math fun and interesting. To improve her natural skills, Donna relies on her parents' willingness to supply the extras not offered in her "normal" daily schedule.

Athletic Skill Improvement

Elliot's parents recognized the importance of skill improvement beyond the "average" for their young athlete. They encouraged his ambition to leave his local recreation soccer team and play instead for a select traveling team. This team played many more games than his school or recreational team, and the level of competition was much higher. In addition, to help Elliot compete with these better players, his parents enrolled him in several soccer clinics throughout the year. All of these opportunities helped Elliot improve his athletic skills.

ABPD Pressures in Japan

The Japanese way of education often means unrelenting pressure on families, biting competition among children, and fiery jealousy among parents. Competitive entrance exams have long been the key to academic and social success in Japan; in recent decades, the race has become so intense that parents are pushing even infants to take the tests. Now the Japanese media are suggesting that the brutal pressure of the education system has driven a young housewife to murder. Mitsuko Yamada was recently arrested for slaying a two-year-old who had passed an entrance exam at an elite kindergarten, while her own daughter failed an initial random drawing to apply. Sociologist and education specialist Gentaro Kawakami concludes, "In Japan these days, we are raising children as if we were training animals" (Coleman, 1999, p. A33).

This same search for instruction geared to a high level of skill improvement would also be appropriate for a young dancer, musician, or vocalist. Many talented performing artists quickly outgrow their early teachers and need to travel great distances to receive advanced lessons from top-level instructors. There are also specialized camps and college programs geared for exceptional artists that allow them to hone their natural abilities.

In all these cases, encouraging new skill acquisition is a perfectly reasonable motive for enrolling children in specialized programs.

Beware the Risks of Achievement by Proxy Distortion in Pursuing Skill Improvement

Even a sound, positive motive like skill improvement can go wrong when the family is in an ABPD situation. Let's look down the road at our math scholar, Donna. Donna will go to a high school her district calls the Academy of Math and Science. Here she will jump ahead to geometry in her freshman year because she has already completed Algebra I. But let's suppose that shortly after the school year begins, her father discovers that there is also an *honors* geometry class, and he insists over the objections of her teacher and the school administrators that his daughter be transferred into this course. Because her father is a very squeaky wheel, Donna is placed in a class that is over her head, and she begins to struggle. Her father then demands more study time at home and hires a private tutor. Donna manages to pass all her tests, but the grades are not the expected and customary A's. Donna's father becomes noticeably disappointed and enraged, and he insists that she quit the tennis team (the only really social and enjoyable part of Donna's schedule) so she will have time to take more precollege mathematics courses at the university. He desperately wants his daughter to improve her math skills and is prepared to push Donna to make it happen. The question here is, Why? Why is it so important to this father that Donna be at the very top of her math class?

The answer is that Donna's father has become mired in an ABPD situation by ignoring ABP guidelines 2 and 4 (see "From Benign to Abusive" in Part One for the complete list). Donna's father is unable to *recognize the child's psychological and physical needs and then make and prioritize decisions based on these requirements rather than on his own wishes, ambitions, and fantasies*. His insistence that Donna could do better, could do more despite her best efforts has placed her in the wrong learning environment and has forced her to give up out-of-school activities she enjoys. On top of all this, Donna's father has forgotten that *children should never feel that parental love is contingent on winning or excelling in any one educational, sporting, career, or social endeavor*. He has conveyed the message that his approval and love are contingently based on the level of her math achievement.

When advanced opportunities for skill improvement cause family friction, deprive children of time to be children, or place them in situations beyond the scope of their capabilities, it is likely that the family has fallen into an ABPD trap.

Motive Two: Supportive Environment

Accomplished children can feel out of place. Because they are different in some ways from the peers in their immediate environment, they can get the idea that they're abnormal or "weird." This is especially true during early adolescence, when children struggle

The Danger of Jumping Ahead

Families should think twice before allowing a child to skip a grade or be placed on a much higher academic level. Even if a child is academically able to hold her own, she is suddenly inserted into a much older, more mature social group. The difference between ten- and twelve-year-olds, or between eleven- and fifteen-year-olds, can be enormous. The younger child often does not have the social skills, maturity, life experience, or "cool" to handle being in a highly competitive, in group–out group kind of society with older kids. In these cases, there is a great risk for ABPD.

so hard to fit in with their peers and be like "everybody else." For this reason, it's often wise to find opportunities for high-achieving children to be in an environment where "everybody else" has similar abilities and interests. A supportive environment assures them they aren't nuts or deviant for choosing Mozart as their favorite musician when others choose the Backstreet Boys. Having friends who also love to play chess or watch musicals can make these activities feel "normal" and OK.

Without this kind of peer support, it can be very difficult for a talented child to pursue her goals with any level of confidence. Peer pressure is so manipulative that it can cause kids to twist themselves in knots to appear "in" even if this means pretending to be dumb or denying a talent. (Even in today's more gender neutral culture with a disappearing glass ceiling, these pressures are more pronounced for girls than for boys.) To prevent this from happening, it makes sense that many parents find schools, camps, clinics, and classes for their children where they can join others who have the same interests.

Imagine two gifted musicians, for example. Student Amadeus attends a school where the music program is very small and weak and definitely for geeks only. Student Ludwig attends a school where the music program is strong and the members are many and proud. Which student is more likely to reach his potential as a musician? Which student is more likely to drop music completely?

The environment in which a child lives with his potential skill has a direct effect on the development of that skill.

Of course not every child can attend a school that caters to her special gifts on a quality level. Very often children and their parents must find supportive programs on their own. In the case of Ryan Peene, for example, there were limited opportunities in his high school to nurture his exceptional leadership abilities. Outside the student government program, public schools sometimes have little to offer in this area. However, this has not kept Ryan from plunging into the world of politics he so loves. Early in his freshman year, Ryan joined the state Teenage Republicans Club and within a year was its president. He contacted local candidates for public office, joining their staffs and becoming an active campaigner. By his junior year, Ryan was the teen cochairman of a national presidential campaign. He also attended leadership conferences in Washington, D.C., such as the National Conservative Student Conference. Because of the credibility of his established political connections, Ryan was soon off to spend his summers as a congressional page in Washington. None of these activities were sponsored by his school.

Although Ryan is very self-motivated, he admits that he could not do all the things he does without the support of his parents. Although the Peenes are not personally involved in politics and have no desire to jump on a campaign trail, they are very proud of their son's accomplishments and have given him the backing he needs to pursue his goals. They have financed his adventures in Washington; they have chauffeured him to meetings, conferences, and seminars; they have played secretary and receptionist at his kitchen-table office. These parents aren't looking to get anything out of Ryan's political aspirations except the satisfaction of knowing that if he should achieve public office, he may be able to contribute positively to the quality of leadership in this country.

Ryan knows no one in his school or even in his town who has any interest in entering the world of politics. In this he appears alone; but the support and encouragement of his parents has guided him to the organizations, programs, activities, and jobs in which he can gain a sense of belonging and positive, reality-based self-esteem and accomplishment.

Without a doubt, to gain the advantage of a supportive environment is an affirmative reason for enrolling children in specialized schools and programs. But even this logical and reasonable motive can become harmful in an ABPD situation.

Projecting Parental Needs

Specialized programs can be most damaging when parents choose them without considering the wishes of the child. It's true that parents often (even most often) know what is best for their child, but this knowledge can get clouded by the parents' own heady dreams

---

Early Russian Training

Piano virtuoso Vladimir Feltsman has performed with virtually every major American orchestra and is an advocate of the special method for developing musical talent that he experienced in his native Russia.

> The biggest advantage of the Russian system is that it starts in early childhood and the training continues through high school. That's not the case here. Most of the Russian-born musicians who made it on any level were trained from age six and up by the absolutely top available teachers. At that stage of their lives, most children are capable of learning the necessary skills quickly and well, be it in language, mathematics, music, or any given discipline. The way the subject is taught the first time is crucial, and the importance of early musical education cannot be stressed enough [quoted in Subotnik, 1997, p. 308].

> Feltsman goes on to advocate special schools for exceptional children: "Certain ideas such as equality and democracy when applied to the social sphere are quite useful. When they are applied to education and to art, however, it leads to mediocrity. If you do not accept the idea that people have different abilities to learn and believe instead that every one is supposed to be equally smart or equally gifted, a real talent development school could never fly. That's why in this country's political climate, that kind of school . . . would become an easy target for demagogues" (p. 314).

---

and aspirations. I have watched as families take their first deliberate step toward ABPD when they place their children in highly specialized and often competitive environments that the kids don't feel very comfortable in.

Suppose that a mother hears about an exceptional summer program at a prestigious university for elementary school children who excel in creative writing. Her nine-year-old, a talented writer, flat-out doesn't want to go. Maybe she doesn't feel competent enough to join a class alongside eighth graders. Or maybe she likes to write, but not enough to wish for advanced training just yet. Or maybe she just doesn't want to give up two weeks of her summer vacation to "more school." Whatever the reason, she makes it clear that she doesn't want to go.

This is the time a parent must ask, What will she gain if I make her go? and What will she lose if she doesn't go? Honest answers to these questions will help the parent avoid an ABPD situation and abide by ABP guideline 2, which advises parents to *recognize the child's psychological and physical needs and then make and prioritize decisions based on these requirements rather than on their own wishes, ambitions, and fantasies.* If the motive for attending a program is to find a supportive environment and make a child feel comfortable with her abilities, the child also has to want to be there.

ABPD Running Rampant

Eleven-year-old Gerald's summer "vacation" was all mapped out for him. He would spend the first two weeks at a residential computer camp on the West Coast. He would then return to his Midwest home just in time for the six-week university drama program. The morning after the final performance of the group's musical show, he was scheduled to begin a two-week soccer camp, which would end two days before school opened. Gerald's parents wanted their son to have a productive summer, but apparently they are overlooking the purpose of a vacation: to enjoy some downtime, regroup, and relax. This fear of "wasting" time is typical of many high-achieving parents with Type A personalities.

Overscheduling

You can also set yourself up for an ABPD situation if you overstuff your child's schedule with too many programs or classes. It's easy to miss the target of finding a supportive and nurturing environment for your child if you find yourself too excited by the many possibilities that are out there. A child who is too busy going from one specialized program to the next doesn't have time or opportunity to learn any one thing really well, never mind making friends and gaining a sense of belonging. The race to the top is not won by those who finish first. It is won by those who delve deeply with great passion into each area that fascinates them.

Missing the Target

The world of select athletic teams gives us many examples of how easy it is to fall into an ABPD trap when looking for a supportive environment. Fourteen-year-old Matthew, for example, is an extremely talented basketball player. So talented, in fact, that the kids on his town recreation league made fun of him for being a show-off, and their parents complained that he was too good to play in that league. Eventually, Matthew left the town league and joined winter, summer, and fall traveling teams made up of players on his skill level. This is where Matthew belongs and where he can feel comfortable playing his hardest. Unfortunately, his father knows so many people on the circuit that he is able to get his son off of teams that begin to lose and on to winning teams that are headed to the national tournaments. Matthew isn't really a member of any team; he is a ringer, an extra player who gets added to rosters at the last minute when a team wins local tournaments and looks for talented backups to take to the next level. Matthew is seeing lots of high-quality playing time, but he is always the new kid who is frequently shunned for bumping another player onto the bench. Once again, Matthew's skill makes him an outsider without friends, team support, or nurturant coaching.

When you sign your child up for a school, camp, class, or program, make sure it is one that will support not only your child's gifts but also the child himself.

Some Summer Fun

"Instead of sitting in classrooms during the summer, some kids may benefit more from mentorships with people who can excite them and address their individual needs. Some students should have the option to attend space camps or hands-on science programs where they can experience the thrill of high-level science in action rather than behind practice algebraic formulas. I'd rather see students who are good writers at writing workshops where they develop their unique talents and submit their best work for publication. This, to me, is far more valuable than gaining more textbook information. It is not that accelerated learning in classes is not good for some academic achievers, but again, in the summer, I would prefer a choice of opportunities that challenge students in different ways and change the learning modes that they encounter during the school year."

Sally M. Reis, Ph.D., president of the National Association for Gifted Children and professor of educational psychology at the University of Connecticut

Motive Three: Elite Exposure

High-achieving children often have high aspirations in highly competitive arenas. Scholars want to go to the best colleges. Performing artists want to perform with renowned companies. Athletes want to compete in the Olympics. They all want professional careers in the top, most elite level of their field. To do this, it is very often necessary to gain public exposure. The fact is, you can more easily navigate your way to the top when the gatekeepers know your name. For this reason, thousands upon thousands of children flock each year to camps, clinics, showcases, and programs to make a name for themselves. Whether this is good or bad is really not the issue. This is how the game is played, and those who follow the rules are more likely to win.

Playing the Exposure Game

Diana Fasano is a softball player from New Jersey who has played the exposure game with skill and success. Diana's goal is to get a scholarship to play her favorite sport at a notable university. To reach this goal, Diana enrolled in a private high school with a reputation for dominating the sport and the headlines. Here she plays twenty-five games during the regular season and another eight during playoffs for the county and state championships (during the last ten years, this school has won the state sectional title ten times and the state championship title five times). Looking for an edge over the thousands of other girls who also attend powerhouse schools across the country, Diana has spent her summers playing for select traveling teams with reputations for attracting college recruiters. She has also attended showcase games and clinics.

Her softball activities the summer before her senior year were scheduled to meet the goals of both skill improvement and exposure. Diana played on a highly competitive team that scheduled twenty-one weeknight games during June and July. On the weekends, Diana attended tournaments and showcases as far afield as Ohio, Pennsylvania, Massachusetts, Virginia, New York, Florida, and South Dakota. She also attended softball camps in New York at Fordham University, Frozen Ropes Camp in White Plains, and at Queens College.

Because Diana's parents helped her be in the right places at the right times where there were college recruiters and scouts as well as exceptional media coverage, she has received letters of interest from twelve schools, including Dartmouth, Columbia, University of Delaware, and Fairfield University, and she has been offered both academic and athletic scholarships. This aspiring athlete feels that her efforts to gain exposure have definitely paid off.

A Scholar's Race

In the same way, many young scholars attend classes, camps, and programs sponsored by notable institutions in hopes of meeting influential people and gaining notoriety. As portrayed in the 1999 movie *October Sky*, it was a national science fair that pushed future

NASA scientist Homer Hick Jr. to build rockets and earn a college scholarship as a teenager. In the same way, competitions like today's Intel International Science and Engineering Fair attract thousands of hopeful scientists and inventors.

Young scholars are seeking ways to distinguish themselves from the crowd for a good reason. John DiBiaggio, the president of Tufts University in Medford, Massachusetts, says his school received 13,500 applications for 1,200 spots in the freshman class in 1999 and accepted fewer than last year. It turned away one-third of the valedictorians who applied and a number of applicants with perfect 1,600 SAT scores (Bronner, 1999). With admission to selective colleges now more competitive than at any other time in the nation's history, it's no wonder that students and their families are scrambling for ways to beat the lengthening odds.

Exposure in the Spotlight

Performing artists, too, need to be in the spotlight to reach their goals. There are camps, competitions, and showcases galore structured to establish reputations for young artists. Carol Vitala gained admission to Manhattan School of Music by winning a name for herself through local, regional, and national piano competitions. Her skill should speak for itself, but with so many talented pianists applying for admission, wearing medals attesting to superior ability has given her a material advantage over others who have not sought this kind of exposure.

When exposure is the goal, tough competition with the best is inevitable. If a child is mentally and physically up to the challenge, attending special programs and activities for the purpose of being seen and making "schmoozing" connections is a perfectly reasonable motive. However, the risk of ABPD exists on several levels when the motive is exposure.

Risky Sacrifice

If a child's parents become too highly invested (both financially and emotionally) in exposure opportunities, they are in danger of moving into the first stage of ABPD: risky sacrifices. When the results are disappointing (as they often are, because in competitive events only a few come out on top), highly invested parents often feel angry and personally cheated. They put much money and time into these high-profile programs and events with the expectation of having something to show for it in the end. In abusive ABPD households, the children are scolded, shamed, or ridiculed for their "poor" performance. But even in many "normal" households, children acutely feel their parents' disappointment and learn to equate parental love only with success.

Objectification

As parents get caught up in the push to make a name for their child, there is also danger of transitioning into the second stage of ABPD: objectification. It becomes easy to objectify the child and peddle a "product" rather than a human being. We learn well our lessons from public relations and advertising: name recognition through constant media attention gets results and sponsorship. So parents scurry around looking for ways to grab a headline—to make news—forgetting that this product has feelings.

Even a casual observer can't help but question the motives of the parents from Massachusetts whose efforts to gain national attention for their son were recently reported in the *Boston Globe*. According to the news article, these parents "alerted the media [of their son's exceptional accomplishments] preparing a three-page advisory worthy of a polished public relations firm" (Farragher,

It's Tough at the Top

Climbing to the higher levels is bound to produce "poor" performances occasionally. Moving up the ladder of ability puts a young star in competition with other stars. In these circumstances, each one is less exceptional in comparison to others, and the child's ability to stand out is lessened. Also, as developmental spikes and valleys allow the competition to catch up, formerly exceptional children can suffer great stress from increased parental expectations. On the elite level, disappointment is inevitable. Some children will never regain the initial glory of early brilliance.

1999, p. B1). They wrote up their own press releases and sent them out to the media because they want the world to know that their son is "at the top of his class. He's an editor, researcher, musician, inventor, entrepreneur, mathematical whiz, role model, scholar, and one heck of a squash player" (p. B1). Before you dash off a press release to the Associated Press, *please* think about the feelings of the "product" you're selling.

Motive Four: Résumé Building

At some time in their lives, high-achieving children will most likely compete for placement in selective schools, classes, camps, and programs. To gain an advantage over other applicants, it is often necessary to show a history of involvement and achievement in one's area of talent—after-school classes, Saturday school, special classes, and specialized summer camps to the rescue.

If your young computer whiz wants to be accepted into the pre-college summer program at a prestigious university, for example, it's generally smart to first enroll him in a local program or two to impress the admissions officers with his background experience and level of interest. If your budding Mozart would like to attend a selective or magnet music school, it's a good idea to first build a credible reputation by joining a high-quality youth orchestra or band, entering notable competitions, and taking advantage of opportunities to perform in concerts and recitals. And if your young Jackie

Premature Exposure

In *Musical Prodigies: Masters at an Early Age* (Fisher, 1973, p. 172), the author tells us, "Of all the things a teacher can do to ruin a prodigy—both his career and in his personal life—the most certain is to rush the student into public appearances before he is ready. Often this is the result of parental or managerial insistence, but the good teacher strives to prevent this disastrous course. Probably more of the failures (far outnumbering the successes) among talented prodigy-musicians have resulted from premature exposure than from any other single cause."

Joyner-Kersee expects college recruiters to believe she has worked hard to build exceptional skills, she'd better be ready to show evidence of experience beyond the typically short schedule in her town league.

For these reasons, attending special programs for the purpose of résumé building is a quite reasonable motive. Unfortunately, when résumé building is the prime motivation behind enrollment in any program, the risk of ABPD is great.

Some admissions officer at some college somewhere must have once said that he looks for students who go the extra mile—and the race was on. This need to build an impressive résumé is the reason that most high-achieving children have no idea what it's like to enjoy idle time. They live in a world driven by high-achieving adults who structure, organize, choreograph, and supervise their every move, afraid to waste a single moment of time. These adults have made the message clear: to make their school records and college applications stand out, today's kids must join, volunteer, do more, do extra, go beyond the norm.

Good Intentions Gone Bad

Before you get caught up in this race, look where you're going, or you may end up with a confused and burned-out child like twelve-year-old Brian. Brian loved his computer. He would spend hours pecking at the keys and thrilling at each new spontaneous discovery he stumbled on. His parents were very supportive and offered to enroll him in a Saturday computer class offered through the local Boys and Girls Club. Brian loved the program so much, his parents began to keep their eyes open for other opportunities. They found after-school programs, Saturday programs, weekend workshops, and summer camps. When Brian began complaining that he didn't want to go to these special programs anymore, his dad told him harshly, "This isn't just for fun, Brian. I've spent a lot of money on these programs so you can get a scholarship to a good school like MIT or Harvard. Do you want to go to a good college or not?"

At the age of twelve, Brian had no idea what he wanted in his future, but he wasn't going to argue the point with his father, so he agreed to fly across the country to attend a residential camp with a national reputation that his father was very excited about. For seven days Brian worked with computer programs from 9 A.M. until 8 P.M. with a one-hour break each lunchtime. It was a very expensive program, and Brian was afraid to tell his parents how much the whole

Special Camps, Classes, and Programs

The four most common reasons for enrolling children in special camps, classes, and programs are neither good nor bad in themselves. The outcome will depend on the child's needs and the parents' motivation.

- Skill improvement
  Pro: Child's talent can be nurtured and guided in constructive directions.
  Con: Too many "extras" can cause family friction, deprive children of time to be children, or place them in situations beyond the scope of their capabilities.
- Supportive environment
  Pro: Provides opportunities for high-achieving children to be in an environment where "everybody else" has similar abilities and interests.
  Con: Children who are too busy going from one specialized program to the next don't have time or the opportunity to make friends and gain a sense of belonging.
- Elite exposure
  Pro: High-achieving children often have high aspirations in highly competitive arenas. To reach their goals, it is very often necessary to gain public exposure.
  Con: It becomes easy to objectify the child and peddle a product rather than a human being.
- Résumé building
  Pro: To gain an advantage over other applicants, it is often necessary to show a history of involvement and achievement in one's area of talent.
  Con: Too many résumé-building activities deprive children of downtime with friends and time to explore the many other dimensions of their lives.

thing really bored him, how much he missed home, and how much all he really wanted to do was go swimming with some friends back home. By the time he returned home, his father was already making contacts to enroll Brian in another computer class.

Brian's parents had begun their search for supportive programs for Brian with all good intentions. But soon they got so wrapped up in making him and themselves look good and in the hope of landing a college scholarship that they lost sight of what Brian wanted and needed. They moved into the ABPD situation of risky sacrifice when they invested so much time and money in Brian's computer education that they broke guideline 7: *allowing the benefits of his achievements to become the primary goal rather than a possible dividend.* They then moved into the second phase of ABPD when they objectified Brian's skill, ignoring guideline 2 that requires parents to *recognize a child's psychological and physical needs and make decisions based on these requirements rather than their own wishes, ambitions, and fantasies.* The father wanted so much for his son to get into a notable college that he forgot that there was a young boy behind the computer skill—a young boy who needed downtime with his friends and time to explore the many other dimensions of himself.

If you are considering adding another activity to your child's list of things to do because you believe it will look good on a résumé, think before you sign. The value of placing an activity on a résumé should be a secondary by-product of its value to your child.

There are many other reasons beyond these four motives for enrolling high-achieving children in specialized classes, schools, programs, and camps. We have offered these as illustrative examples to give you an idea of how to judge the good and bad aspects of a decision to sign up for any special school or out-of-school program.

ADVICE FROM THE EXPERTS

People who are closely involved with specialized programs have seen it all. They've seen talented young children blossom in a supportive environment, and they've seen bullied children burn out from the stress. We have interviewed two experts to find out what they have to say about the value of a specialized school, class, camp, or program for the development of a child's potential. They are (1) Jack DiSalvo, coach and author of the book *College Admissions for the High School Athlete* and (2) Dr. Ralph Opacic, executive director of the Orange County High School of the Arts.

Athletics

Jack DiSalvo, who has twenty-eight years' experience as a secondary school athletic instructor, coach, and adviser, was named Coach of the Year by the *New York Daily News,* and has received the National High School Coaches Award from *Scholastic Coaches Magazine.* In his book, *College Admissions for the High School Athlete* (Facts on File, 2000), DiSalvo advises athletes and parents to take advantage of opportunities for skill improvement, exposure, and experience—with caution. We asked him what young athletes and parents should know about noninterscholastic sporting camps, clinics, showcases, and leagues.

"Some camps and clinics are primarily instructional. They are staffed by experienced athletes and coaches, and they focus on physical conditioning, skill-related workouts, educational films, lectures, and academic counseling. Others are simply showcases. They do little more than put kids together to compete before college coaches, recruiters, and scouts.

"Both instructional and showcase camps have their advantages and disadvantages, depending on an athlete's needs. Instructional camps are the most worthwhile for younger athletes who are still perfecting skills. But they don't attract many recruiters, and junior- and senior-year athletes may find the clinic-type atmosphere boring. Showcase camps offer more opportunities to compete and show off, which can help an athlete build a reputation and judge his or her capabilities against the barometer of other athletes who also hope to compete on the college level.

"When choosing a showcase camp, beware. Many of the biggest and most publicized camps recruit the nation's top high school athletes in the hope of attracting more college recruiters. Then they fill the majority of slots with less talented campers who pay top dollar to be overshadowed by the superstars. It's not that the less talented athletes don't have the ability to compete in college; it's just that, because the competitions at camps are often quick and unstructured, the recruiters are distracted by the big name participants.

"A talented athlete can also gain experience and exposure by competing in noninterscholastic leagues and tournaments. This is a good move especially if your child competes in a weak or little-known conference. There are many opportunities, especially during the off season, to compete in leagues and tournaments that offer better competition, that push athletes to excel beyond their school level, and that give a realistic view of individual skills. Before you sign up your athlete, however, consider three things:

"First is the level of competition. Before you sign up for a camp, investigate the caliber of athletes who are involved in the program. To ensure a high level of competition, do athletes try out for a spot? Is it invitational so that only other skilled athletes participate? Or is it open to anyone so that the level will span from so-so to very talented? It's counterproductive for young athletes to spend time and effort working out with or competing against athletes consistently below their level. But it's also risky to jump into a level too far ahead. The talented athlete who struggles to keep up with the blue-chippers can not only lose confidence but also lose positive recruiting opportunities. Going to 'the best' camp or tournament is not always the best choice. You should seek a level where the competition is challenging but fair.

"Second, you should consider the potential for exposure. Noninterscholastic athletic programs can be fun and educational, but once your child has set intercollegiate competition as the ultimate goal, the who-will-see-me factor becomes a major consideration when choosing one program over another. Because some activities are geared primarily toward instruction and others toward exposure, when you inquire about a program, ask which one you can expect.

"And third, consider the cost. Exposure can be the most expensive factor in the college recruiting process, so it certainly needs to be considered when evaluating athletic programs. The answer to the question, What is the cost of exposure? depends on your goals. If you expect to attend a local Division III state college, it's not necessary to spend thousands of dollars to go camp and tournament hopping around the country. Local college coaches are likely to attend high school events if they're notified that an athlete is interested in being recruited; they are also more likely to attend area off-season events, where local athletes can be evaluated without their spending a fortune. On the other hand, if you hope to get a full scholarship to a highly competitive Division I college, you may decide, for example, that a $3,000 investment in athletic programs across the country may be worth the return in scholarships valued at $80,000."

Performing Arts

Fourteen years ago, Dr. Ralph Opacic wrote a grant request to fund a public performing arts high school in southern California. Today he is executive director of the Orange County High School of the Arts. We asked him what the benefit is of sending a talented child to a school or program that specializes in the arts.

"The direct or obvious reason that parents consider sending their children to a specialized school is that the students get significantly more hours of instruction and a higher level of instruction in their area of specialty. Our students have an extended high school day that adds three hours onto the schedule each day

Choosing an Athletic Program for Elite Exposure

Consider the level of competition. The exact level of any athletic event is difficult to assess, but you should make an effort to get a general idea before you sign up. Ask program organizers to define the level of competition at their events and ask for the phone numbers of athletes who have participated in the program in the past. Most young athletes are quite willing to share their experiences and may in the end be your best source for an honest appraisal. Finally, if you have the time and opportunity to observe the program at an earlier session, this too will give you insight into the participants' competitive level.

Consider the potential for exposure. Be very direct in getting this information by asking program organizers for specific details: "Do college coaches attend your program for the purpose of recruiting?" "What colleges sent representatives last year?" "Who do you expect will be there this year?" If competing on a college level is your child's goal, it's foolish to spend time, money, and sweat on athletic programs that nobody knows about. When choosing noninterscholastic sports activities, be sure to calculate exposure potential into your decision-making formula.

Consider the cost. If you talk to athletes who have spent money on exposure camps and showcases and have won scholarships, you'll hear that the programs are worth every penny. If you talk to those who have spent large sums on exposure opportunities and didn't land lucrative scholarships, they'll tell you it's a waste of money. That's why the bottom line on putting down big bucks on noninterscholastic athletic events is that it's a gamble. If you spend the money now on top-notch programs, you might get it back (and more) in scholarship dollars, but then again you might not.

for instruction in their art area. I think traditional high schools tend to have only an introductory, experiential approach to the arts. Specialized schools have a more intensive, comprehensive program to prepare kids for professional work or for entering an art college experience. That's the direct benefit.

"There are also secondary benefits that go along with it. The students often tell me that in their other schools they didn't have a supportive peer group. Because they have such passion for the arts, they missed having a group of people who appreciated their talent and the self-discipline it takes to be committed to a goal. At specialized schools the students have a peer group that encourages them, inspires them, and challenges them. Grouping kids who share the same level of interest is one of the key elements of any good specialized school.

"Another benefit is the quality of the staff at specialized schools and the connections they offer to the outside world. Very often these teachers are more experienced and professional than you'll find in other schools. Nearly all of our staff have been or are working in the professional arts industries. This builds a natural connection between the school and the artistic community. Our theatrical directors and choreographers, musicians, and dancers who are a part of the working arts world are able to help our students make that step from high school to the workplace. That is another advantage that naturally evolves out of specialized programs. One of our successful alums who is working on Broadway in New York right now will tell you that having been here and having the experience and the exposure to professional artists and teachers and the support of her peer group put her five to ten years ahead of everyone else in terms of launching her career.

"Whenever families invest a lot of time and often money in specialized programs, there are expectations of some kind of return for the effort. If the student is focused and serious about her instruction, you should be able to see signs of maturity and growth in her skill development. You have a right to expect that. If you don't see that, you have a right to investigate and ask why not. If it's not because the student isn't motivated anymore, you need to find some other place where you will see that the child is growing and challenged.

"At the same time, everyone has to understand that there are absolutely no guarantees. There are students who go through our school showing tremendous talent and ability, but out in the real world they don't get that big break they're looking for. The students and families should make their investments and commitments for the personal benefit they give to the student as a whole person. We've had students who have left here wanting to be actors or singers and then end up in a completely different field, but I honestly believe that the time and energy they spent in this school wasn't wasted. The value of the self-discipline, peer support, and commitment they learn here will help them in any field they venture into."

Part-Time Elite Instruction

If your talented child doesn't have the opportunity to attend a specialized school, you can find high-quality programs that are run during the summers or on weekends that give performing artists the support, high-quality instruction, and exposure they need. Thirteen-year-old Dana, for example, is one of thousands of young dancers on the professional dance track who come out to Los Angeles every summer and stay in hotels with their families while taking classes at a professional dance studio. Many talented young artists who do not attend specialized school get exposure and experience by joining youth orchestras and opera companies, and local community theaters.

Special children need special opportunities to grow, experiment, discover, and investigate their strengths and weaknesses. The schools, classes, camps, and programs across the country that cater to these needs make a valuable contribution to the overall development of an exceptional child—if the parents stay on the right side of the line that separates supportive parenting from ABPD. Step Three will help you identify where to draw that line when dealing with a child's teacher, mentor, or coach.

Step Three

Beware Abusive Instructors

Nurturing a high-achieving child in athletics, academics, or the performing arts should be a team effort. The team members include the child, the parents, and the coaches, tutors, teachers, and mentors. The interplay between this group of team members has a strong influence on the potential for nurturing happy, healthy, and sane high-achieving children.

The goal of this team dynamic should be to keep the inevitably unbalanced power of the team members in some sort of equilibrium. As we have seen, however, Achievement by Proxy Distortion (ABPD) too often creates a pressure disturbance or perturbation in the system that puts the child at risk for physical, mental, and emotional harm. In previous chapters, we have discussed many examples of overly ambitious parents whose personal, overriding need for attention and achievement drives them to exploit their own children. In this chapter, we'll take a look at the most common ways that instructors too can fall into ABPD traps. We'll see the dangers that occur when parents relinquish their responsibilities to instructors whose own ambitions can lead to a loss of perspective, inappropriate expectations, excessive competitive pressures, and even various forms of exploitation and abuse. In these ABPD situations, there is a clear loss of the instructor's ability to differentiate his own physical and psychological needs from a child's developmental needs and goals. The involved adult is at risk for crossing the line from risky sacrifice, through objectification, toward potential abuse.

This progression through the stages of ABPD occurs when instructors violate the ABPD guidelines discussed in "From Benign to Abusive" in Part One. Especially vulnerable to instructor abuse are guidelines 2, 3, 6, and 7:

- Guideline 2: *Instructors should be able to recognize the child's psychological and physical needs, then make and prioritize decisions based on these requirements rather than on their own wishes, ambitions, and fantasies.*

  Example: A certain music teacher is establishing a reputation for sending the best violinists to a renowned summer camp. This year, her most talented student doesn't want to go to the camp, and the teacher has begun badgering her and hinting that she is not really dedicated to her music or worthy of her position as first violinist in the local youth orchestra. This teacher feels she needs this student to attend the camp to maintain her own reputation—not because it would benefit the child.

- Guideline 3: *Instructors should be able to distinguish between their own feelings of anger and disappointment (as well as their pride and pleasure) and the child's feelings; they should not project their own feelings onto the child.*

  Example: When a young scholar shows his tutor the disappointing results of his exam, the histrionic tutor tears up the paper, throws it in the garbage, and storms out of the room slamming the door behind him. This tutor has lost the ability to recognize whose failure and disappointment should be the prime consideration at this moment.

- Guideline 6: *Instructors should encourage developmentally appropriate independence, autonomy, and decision-making skills in children. They should not, however, hide behind that independence when important, even critical, decisions are to be made.*

  Example: A young swimmer has a bad ear infection and has been advised by her doctor to stay out of the water for one week. The coach needs this swimmer to compete in an important single elimination meet two days from now. However, he does not want to be accused of jeopardizing her health, so his covert strategy becomes to put the decision in her hands. He tells her, "The team is really counting on you, but I don't want you to swim unless you feel well enough to do it." He (and her parents, who blindly concur with the charismatic coach's words) is giving her inappropriate decision-making power, which I call pseudoautonomy.

- Guideline 7: *Social and financial benefits of the child's achievements should be a dividend, rather than a primary goal for the instructor.*

  Example: A tennis coach who earns a living by taking a percentage of her student's winnings finds herself in financial trouble. Her solution is to enter her top players in more and more tournaments to increase the odds of her earning income. This will require them to miss more school than originally agreed; they will be away from their families for longer periods of time, and they will play more often than is physically safe. In cases like this, exploitative financial gain rather than the child's appropriate development or achievement is the primary goal.

All these cases beg the question, Where are the parents?! To prevent a child from entering into a risky "carte blanche" relationship with an instructor, the parents must assertively stay in charge and be on the lookout for signs that the instructor is at risk for ABPD. The following five instructor profiles will give you an idea of the kinds of signs to look for. You may find all five traits in one instructor; you may find only one, and to a rather mild degree; or happily you may find none at all in your child's instructor. The point is to be aware of these ABPD types so you can stay in charge of your child's growth and development.

Avoiding the Win-at-Any-Cost Instructor

Some instructors of athletes, scholars, and performing artists know how to get results. They build renowned reputations for creating winners, so it is considered a privilege and an honor to train with them—even though it is well known that they are tough taskmasters.

I have seen firsthand how the strong reputation of these instructors encourages parents to overlook the fact that they often cut corners to get those impressive results. This is the kind of coach who may allow or tacitly encourage his athletes to get involved with steroids, blood doping, performance-enhancing drugs, and various other unethical training methods while denying any awareness of the practices, using the defensive rationalization known as plausible deniability. This instructor will encourage dancers, gymnasts, and wrestlers to drop weight beyond healthy boundaries. This teacher will ignore the headaches, stomachaches, and more debilitating signs of anxiety and stress of young scholars under pressure. The process of gaining skill, experience, and knowledge is not what's important to these instructors. Rising to the top and being the "best" is all that matters.

The Price of Success

Because this instructor builds a personal reputation on the success of her students, he is at constant risk of being in an ABPD situation. The controversial gymnastics coach Bela Karolyi is an interesting example. Karolyi coached all but one of the six national champions between 1987 and 1992. He gained world fame as the coach of Mary Lou Retton, Kim Zmeskal, Kerri Strug, and Dominique Moceanu. Who can argue with such a record of success? What young gymnast wouldn't be thrilled to be his student?

Yet Karolyi's methods have often been questioned. He has been accused of pushing his athletes too far, calling them names, and taunting them about being fat. It was one of Karolyi's protégés, Kerri Strug, who clinched the gold medal with her gutsy (but as it turned out unnecessary) second vault after he encouraged her to "shake it off" when she sprained her ankle. Likewise, when Betty Okino suffered stress fractures in her back shortly before the 1992 Olympic trials, Karolyi reportedly accused her of being soft, motivating her to go back into the gym and qualify for the Olympic squad. Tough and risky (potentially causing lifelong disability or deformity), but effective.

Karolyi's tactics are glossed over despite public awareness of his questionable coaching style. But that doesn't mean he's not admired. Strug initially bristled at the mere suggestion that Karolyi pressured her into making the second vault: "Bela is a very tough coach and he gets criticism for that," she says. "But that's what it takes to become a champion" (Associated Press, 1996, p. 2). In con-

Stay in Charge!

This is your child—you are the parent. When you confront a win-at-any-cost instructor, you have to assert yourself, not be passive, and take charge. This can be very difficult when instructors who allege to have more expertise and experience than you put incredible pressures on you or your children. Ultimately, what is best for your child is *your* call, as long as it is safe and nurturing.

trast, Bart Conner, who won a gold medal as part of the 1984 men's squad and is now married to Nadia Comaneci, says, "Bela knows only one speed and that's full-blast forward. He goes full-blast until they crash. It's hard for him to back off and nurture a kid" (p. 73).

Many children are raised believing that the most important thing in the world is to be a champion athlete, scholar, or performing artist. They willingly do whatever it takes to achieve this goal. They and their parents gradually come to believe that the end justifies the means. Parents reason, "This is the person who has a proven history of competence. This is the person who can make my child's dreams come true. Other children have worked with him without harm; my child deserves the opportunity to work with the best too." Each new winner to emerge from the group feeds the ambition and desire of the others to continue the grueling regimen and become one of the best. They endure the pain and the hardships, hoping to come out ahead with the prize, money, recognition, or whatever else the goal may be. When the gold ring is grasped, the instructor becomes a virtual god. Where there is ambition and the potential for high-level success, parents, children, and their instructors often make a deal with the devil in exchange for the greater possibility of success—and damn the high risks.

Where to Draw the Line

Because it is so easy to get caught up in the quest for success, you must make a conscious effort to stay in charge of your child's health and well-being and to be alert to the signs of ABPD. You must know in advance that you will draw a line in the sand and intervene the

Getting an Objective Opinion

It's often difficult to know when a child is being pushed too hard by an instructor, especially when the child insists, "I want to do it." If you have a gut feeling that the training process is too grueling or is endangering the physical or mental health of your child, consider family counseling. It often helps to sit down with a therapist who can objectively evaluate what's going on and offer both you and your child guidelines and advice for pursuing a goal in a safe manner.

moment you see your child being subject to unnecessary risk, neglect, exploitation, or abuse. The following sections describe some of the most obvious objectionable practices encouraged by instructors who believe that the end justifies any means.

Putting Children in Risky Situations

Is it risky to have a nine-year-old chess player travel, board, and spend unsupervised time with older teen players? Is it risky to ask a child TV actor to do an underwater drowning scene that has the potential to "go wrong"? Is it risky to require teen athletes, dancers, and skaters to train more than thirty hours per week? There are not always simple yes or no answers to these questions. Dangerous situations are usually called risky only in retrospect, when something has gone wrong. If tragedy had not struck, the headlines would not have asked us to consider whether the father of seven-year-old Jessica Dubroff or the complicitous sponsors and media put her at risk by allowing her to pilot a cross-country plane trip, or whether the Ramsays were asking for trouble by sexualizing six-year-old Jon Benet in beauty pageants, as do many other "pageant parents." It's our job as parents to keep an eye open for signs of *potential* danger and to be willing to speak out when we find it.

In earlier chapters, we have seen that in order to protect children from risky situations, parents must be able to separate their own needs from their child's needs. Now we can see that the parents must also make sure that the child's instructor can do the same. If you feel that your child's health or emotional well-being is being endangered in the pursuit of perfection and success, it is absolutely

Safety First

Sir Ernest Shackleton, the Antarctic explorer of the early 1900s, has a reputation for being able to differentiate between the desire for glory and the sometimes contradictory need for safety (as opposed to other explorers, such as Robert Falcon Scott, who died in 1912 after reaching the pole, and Roald Amundsen, who was first to the pole). In 1907, Shackleton turned back just ninety miles short of reaching the pole because he thought the odds of men dying were just too high. On another North Pole adventure between 1914 and 1916, Shackleton overcame astonishing odds and returned with his men "from the dead" when his boat was crushed by pack ice.

necessary (but admittedly difficult) to immediately step in and take charge.

In my practice, I have noticed that this is especially true for athletes and performing artists. Their instructors are notoriously guilty of walking a thin line between pushing to perfection and pushing over the edge. Do not tolerate any coach who encourages the use of performance-enhancing drugs; pathogenic behaviors, such as bulimia or food or fluid restriction; or methods of rapid fluid weight loss, such as sweating in garbage bags or sitting in saunas. And always be alert to signs of overtraining. Now that children tend to specialize in one area of performance at a young age and perform year round, using the same groups of muscles again and again, they are more at risk for overuse injuries. Coaches must be caring enough and knowledgeable about the physical development of children to understand that some children may not be developed fully enough to handle repetitive activities that place excessive stress on the developing musculoskeletal system. The young baseball pitcher who throws too many difficult pitches, the young dancer who does too many deep-knee bends, or the young soccer player who heads too many balls is at risk for injuries that may sabotage development into a healthy, mature performer and person.

It is not appropriate for parents to take all decision-making power away from the instructor. But if you see that a particular instructor is a win-at-all-costs kind of person, stay highly vigilant

> ## Inappropriate on Any Level
>
> "The playing fields have become flooded with coaches behaving as if they've just attended a Bobby Knight School of Intimidation. Organized sports have become fertile ground for coaches with bulging veins, foul mouths, clenched fists, and volatile tempers. These are coaches who seem to model their behavior after Vince Lombardi's outdated overused creed, 'Winning isn't everything, it's the only thing.' This may be fine at the professional level, but totally inappropriate for kids' sports—on any level."
>
> *Fred Engh, founder and president of*
> *the National Alliance for Youth Sports*

and watch for questionable practices, advice, and situations. Be prepared to intervene and say, "No more. Your verbally abusive, negative coaching style just does not mesh with my child's personality. We're going elsewhere; the potential for damage is just not worth it." Meanwhile, continue to consult with outside, more objective and trustworthy observers who may see you "morphing" into a win-at-all-costs parent. Remember that your child is with that coach *only* because of your permission and choice.

Forcing Children to Perform Even When They Are Injured

Would your child's instructor expect your child to perform bravely when injured? If you suspect that she would, it's time to reassess the value of this instructor. She could be in an ABPD trap that will end up hurting your child. However, even if you feel that your child's instructor would never force or convince anyone to perform when sick or injured, don't let that feeling make you complacent. It is a rare few who blatantly abuse their students. You won't often hear "I don't care how sick you are; get out there and perform." Most sidestep this direct kind of abuse by putting the decision in the hands of the child.

They will say, as in a case we mentioned earlier, "If you don't feel you can do it, then don't." These instructors know that high achievers will risk everything to please the coach and their parents. They also know that a child can distance or dissociate herself from her

The Antisocial or Sociopathic Instructor

Some instructors are conscienceless, selfish individuals who reject any responsibility to maintain appropriate relationship boundaries. They are likely to involve others in ways that serve any selfish or inappropriate desire. Exploitation of others is routine. Often these individuals are not exposed until they have left a trail of emotionally traumatized victims. Parents of victims, and adults who were violated during their adolescence, can and sometimes do take legal action to expose these individuals. Unfortunately, many of the injured refuse to take action because of the emotional and social pain that would be a consequence of public exposure. When interviewed, young women or men have expressed anger, embarrassment, shame, and guilt that as complicit victims they may have not acted in their own best interest even over an extended period of abuse (Ogilvie, Tofler, Conroy, and Drell, 1998). (Although the term *sociopath* is commonly understood in lay literature, you'll find that in medical literature it has recently been replaced by the term *antisocial*.)

own body. She objectifies it as if the body belonged to somebody else, and she is not concerned when the body is in danger, when it aches, when it's injured, when it's tortured with excessive eating, dieting, fitness, or training regimens. This is why a child should not have to deal with questions that force her to make an important decision: "Do you feel strong enough to perform with that stress fracture in your vertebra?" Even in normal circumstances, children are not mature or informed enough to understand the long-term health consequences of their actions; in the realm of elite performers who have objectified their bodies, the instructor is almost always guaranteed, indeed demands, a yes response. In these cases, achieving one's personal best has been traded in for the far less noble pursuits of today's ultracompetitive, high-pressure, do-anything-it-takes-to-win world.

You must also be on the lookout for instructors who risk a child's health out of ignorance. This is especially important when young athletes and performing artists work with instructors who haven't had any type of formal training in youth instruction or child development. Although they may be highly skilled themselves, these people are more likely to teach techniques inappropriate for young bodies; fail to conduct proper warm-up, cool-down, and stretching exercises; neglect to provide relevant instruction in important areas, and send children out to perform without taking necessary safety precautions.

Going for All or Nothing

There are many win-at-any-costs instructors who require total control of the children they guide to success. They make it clear to the parents that if they agree to accept the child into their program, they must have complete freedom to make all decisions regarding the child's training and future. Typical of this situation is one case in which a tennis instructor thought he had found a future champion in a sixteen-year-old boy named Tim. He offered to continue lessons with Tim at no charge to the family with the stipulation that he would control over managing Tim's career. The instructor volunteered to give his undivided attention to Tim if the family allowed him to make all the significant decisions about Tim's life as a competitor. This was an offer the parents, and particularly the domineering father, felt they could not refuse. This kind of deal is also a red flag of a win-at-any-cost instructor with major ABPD problems.

Don't Take His Word for It

You can't always believe what an instructor tells you. Look deeper. A wrestling coach may say, "I would never tell my boys to sweat off weight and jeopardize their health." But he will tell his boys, "You've got to do everything you can to stay at 135 pounds if you want to be the best. Talk to the older kids; they'll help you with your weight." This kind of coach doesn't give specific dangerous instructions, but he knows the older kids will advise steroids and vomiting. He is deluding himself and others with rationalizations that allow him plausible deniability and grant pseudoautonomy to the children in his charge— a sure sign of a coach in the objectification stage of ABPD.

Instructors have the right to ask parents to back off and trust their expertise, but they never have the right to take complete control of a child's life—even when the promise of success is so tempting. In a recent *Newsweek* article ("Life in Romania," 1999), Olympic gymnast Kerri Strug gave us more information about her training with Bela Karolyi. With three years of perspective, she admitted, "Bela had complete control of everything in your life—your workouts, your eating, your sleeping. . . . I look back now and say, 'That was crazy. That's not America.' But it was Bela's way or no way. And he was a coach who got you where you wanted to go" (p. 73). Karolyi fulfills his promise to a handful of resilient hopefuls like Strug and Dominique Moceanu every four years, making it look like his dictatorial methods are worth it, but what about the five hundred other young girls who train at his summer camp each year? Do they look back and think that those months of isolation without family or visitors or even phone calls were worth it? When choosing a win-at-any-cost instructor who requires total control of the child, families have to agonize long and hard over whether the ends really will justify the means, especially, as in most cases, when the child does not come out on the very top. (See Step Four for more information regarding the sacrifices of high-level training.)

Winning Really Isn't Everything

There are very reputable and successful instructors for athletes, scholars, and performing artists who do not subscribe to the win-at-all-costs mentality. These are people who understand that success can also be attained when children challenge themselves to compete against their own personal best—not the rest of the world. This emphasis on the process of task-oriented personal improvement has several advantages over focusing solely on winning: it creates less pressure and more enjoyment, and allows children and their parents and coaches to feel good about themselves regardless of the outcome on any particular day.

If you think this kind of task-oriented training sounds too simplistic and idealistic for building a champion, consider that, paradoxically, taking the emphasis off winning has been proven to be an effective way to actually create a winner. When a child focuses on an internal variable such as effort, rather than an external one such as outcome, he experiences an increased sense of self-efficacy or control. Because feeling in control of oneself and one's destiny is one of the psychological characteristics of peak achievement states, often referred to as *flow* or *being in the zone,* learning to focus inwardly on effort can lead to more effective performance—and therefore increase the likelihood of winning!

Watch the people whom you allow to guide your children. If you see signs of a dictator who has no personal interest in an individual child's needs or skills beyond those that he or she deems necessary to winning, and who seems to treat your child more like a product than a person, it's time to find a new instructor. There are many wonderful instructors who are not caught up in an ABPD win-at-any-cost trap and are able to see the children they teach as individuals. They are flexible and use teaching methods that match the temperament and needs of each child. They work with child and family to get the best results without being abusive. They will also tolerate mistakes as part of the learning process, without being "losers"; they take the opportunity to learn and teach when your child misses the mark and are prepared to risk loss in order to nurture and protect your child from undue risk even when the stakes are high.

Defining Success for Young Athletes

A recent study in Europe (Escarti, Roberts, Cervello, and Guzman, 1999) researched the influence of parents, coaches, and peers on how young athletes define success in sports. The athletes were asked to identify success as either (1) performing better than others and winning, or (2) applying effort and making progress and showing mastery in their own performance. Parents, coaches, and peers were asked to do the same. The study concluded that when parents, coaches, and peers view success as winning rather than personal mastery, the athlete feels the same. The authors confirmed that "significant others serve as a mirror through which we judge our criteria for success in sport."

The Burden of the Star Maker

Exceptionally talented children often compete in programs along with children of average or limited talent. This is usually the case in town recreational programs and in public school programs. There is nothing inherently wrong or abusive about this situation; it is what the instructor *does* with the more talented children that determines whether the children's "risk factor" of exceptional talent places these kids in an ABPD situation.

Instructors who see these children as individuals with special needs for higher-level instruction and performance can do a great deal to nurture children's talents and encourage sustained success. But instructors who see these children as a ticket to personal fame and recognition might turn them into "stars" and use them to make themselves look good—and this can be dangerous for the kids.

The Burden of Being the Best

In the case of eleven-year-old Dan, for example, his baseball coach quickly realized that he could ride Dan to a championship. At first, stars like Dan (and their closely identifying parents) feel flattered by the praise and attention. They feel special that the instructor tells everyone to watch them. They feel proud when they single-handedly win a game. But soon the pressure of carrying the team can become excessive. Dan can't sit out an inning when he is hurt; he can't miss a game when he is sick; he can never skip a game to go with his family to an amusement park or on a vacation. The coach makes it very clear that the team needs him. "You can't miss a game!" he bellows. "You have to be here or we'll lose!" The other teammates tend to resent Dan because he attracts all the coach's attention and praise, and he never has to sit on the bench occasionally like everyone else, but at the same time they would get angry at him if he were to miss a game and cause them to lose. Soon Dan feels totally responsible for the fate of the team. If he makes an error in the field or strikes out at bat, the coach, the fans, and his teammates loudly show their disappointment—Dan is not supposed to let them down. Dan begins to notice that when Bobby hits a single, everyone cheers, but when he hits one, everyone complains it wasn't a double. He notices that when the other pitchers walk a batter, the coaches say, "That's OK; you'll get the next one." But when he walks a batter, they say, "What's the matter with you! We needed that out!" Dan is no longer a member of the team—he *is* the team. Dan's coach has created an ABPD situation. He has lost sight of Dan the young boy struggling to do his best and understand the "contingent love" that is based on his performance. He sees only the talent that can make him a winning coach in the short term and justify to himself and others the sacrifices that he may have to make.

This is excessive pressure that only few children can handle, physically or emotionally. Many come to find their "talent" causes them great anxiety. They worry constantly. They question their ability to always win. They can suffer the physical consequences of unrelenting stress: insomnia; headaches and stomachaches, which in more extreme cases become migraines; chronic fatigue syndrome; chronic pain syndromes, such as fibromyalgia or ulcers; and even conversion disorders, such as pseudoseizures or hysterical loss of the use of a limb, which afford a physical or legitimate "way out" for an overtaxed and overdriven child. (See Step Six for discussion of the warning signs of ABPD.)

Taking Action

High-achieving athletes, scholars, and performing artists all experience some degree of the star syndrome at some point. The ABPD danger lies in how severe and unrealistic the parent-instructor-child milieu is and how long the situation is allowed to continue.

If you see your child in the star situation, you have two possible choices: you can begin by speaking with the instructor and request that your child be treated equally with his peers and not as a saving grace. If this doesn't change the situation, you should find another instructor, preferably on a higher level if your child is developmentally and socially ready for that situation.

The star syndrome is far less likely to occur if your child is placed with other children of similar talent. Private schools, single-sex schools (in particular for talented girls), Saturday university programs, select elite sport teams, and large city gifted-and-talented or performing arts programs are great equalizers. If they are run properly, children can be challenged to improve and to take risks within a more understanding and empathic peer group in which they can grow normally without fear of letting everyone down if they make a mistake.

Understanding the Verbal Batterer

Different instructors use different tactics to motivate children to work hard. Two common tactics are known to be effective, yet they use opposite strategies.

Some instructors motivate children to give their best and to work hard by offering praise and rewards when the children grasp certain tasks or processes. These instructors want children to enjoy their talent because it's fun and because it makes them special. They believe that if a child loves what she does, she will do it longer and better than if she is forced to do something that she considers a dreaded drudgery.

Some instructors teach children to work harder by subjecting them to loud, negative, degrading, and disruptive verbal assaults that follow any fault or flaw. They yell at children when they make a mistake. They taunt and ridicule children who do not rise up to meet the mark. These instructors don't really care about how children will feel about their talent in ten years; they care only how they perform today. These instructors are always at risk for ABPD because they generally put their own needs and emotions before those of the children they instruct.

You have certainly seen both kinds of instructors, but the verbal batterers are the most visible and memorable, and also the most malignant—despite what we see and hear in the media. The celebrity spotlight shows us many examples of verbally aggressive, even borderline abusive, parents and coaches whose children emerge triumphant. We know the story of Tiger Woods's father, Earl, who used marine training techniques like shouting orders and taunting to psychologically "toughen up" eight-year-old Tiger. We've heard about Richard Williams, the father of tennis stars Venus and Serena, who sought to "toughen up" his daughters by asking fans to boo them and have them play only male, stronger opponents. We've watched college and professional coaches of adults, such as Bobby Knight and P. J. Carlesimo, brutally berate not only their own players but also officials and opponents. Knight, Carlesimo, the Williams sisters, and Tiger Woods win games, and that carries a lot of weight in today's society. These high-profile cases of negative coaching strategies send out a message that has trickled down to the instructors who teach our children: yell, scream, ridicule, and embarrass if you want to create a "mentally tough" winner.

Behind the Scenes

Because athletic events are loud, in-your-face events, we have many opportunities to witness this kind of behavior on the athletic field, but there's no doubt that there are many instructors in the performing arts and even in academics who motivate with anger, ridicule, and arbitrary withdrawal of praise in a form of performance-contingent love. Many professional dancers, musicians, and scholars have vivid memories of the hours of behind-the-scene verbal abuse they endured almost as an inevitable rite of passage similar to hazing.

College physics major Troy recalls, "I remember going to my tutor with my knees shaking. I was so afraid of his temper tantrums, and I couldn't stand being called 'stupid' and 'lazy' every time I made a mistake." Clara, a twenty-year-old dancer, also remembers being afraid of an angry instructor: "I would tell my mother that I didn't want to go to my lessons because my teacher was so mean and because she would yell at me and make fun of me, but the teacher

Taking the Fun out of Sports

A study by the Minnesota Amateur Sports Commission reported that 45.3 percent of the children surveyed said adults had called them names, yelled at them, and insulted them while the youngsters played in a sports contest. It also revealed that 21.5 percent had been pressured to play with an injury. Shockingly, 17.5 percent even reported that an adult had hit, kicked, and slapped them while participating in sports (Engh, 1999).

had a good reputation, and lots of kids from my school went there also, so my mom just couldn't believe that it was really that bad."

For most kids, verbal abuse and the threat of physical abuse can be motivational in part because they tap directly into our survival-oriented "fight or flight" arousal neurological responses, which we also use to deal with trauma. This negative motivation can enhance concentration, focus, and energy and drive children to achieve an exemplary performance. But such kids are unlikely to derive life-long pleasure from the activity; they often quit at the earliest possible opportunity. Others, terrified of error or abusive tirades, may choke up as they strive for the impossible. The psychological development of children and youth can be severely impaired by this type of coaching.

If you see evidence that your child's instructor motivates with verbal abuse, don't hesitate to speak up or walk out. Remember that your child's sense of how valuable she is as a person is always more important than how happy your child makes a verbally abusive instructor, no matter how famous or charismatic he may be.

The Teen Years

Even if a child quietly submits to critical abuse in the early stages of training, she may rebel as she reaches her teens. Adolescents are more often motivated by comments that support their sense of autonomy and their sense of self within an accepting peer group than by critical comments they perceive as intended to control them. Also, as their greater discriminatory powers develop, adolescents become more able to judge the appropriateness of the feedback they receive. Feedback should be based on performance, with praise offered when appropriate and corrective instruction offered when warranted (Libman 1998). Teens who have been emotionally abused for years often decide with great relief to abandon their particular field of talent. They feel that not only their failures but also their successes belong to others! This causes a great alienation or dissociation from this part of themselves that may never be resolved.

The Power of a Wise Instructor

In his autobiography, Isaac Stern, one of the most celebrated violinists of the twentieth century, recalls with fondness his violin teacher, Naoum Blinder:

> He was never dogmatic, never rude, never caustic. He spoke with an inherent dignity. His was a kind of benign strength. He didn't stamp out a student's personal approach to music so that one recognized the teacher, not the student. He was an astonishingly strong personality, without any trace of the egotistical about him. He encouraged me to follow my instincts and would stop me only when he felt I was doing something wrong. In other words, he let me develop my own voice on my instrument. His way of teaching became the forming ethic of my whole musical life. He taught me how to teach myself, and for that I will always be grateful. He was the single most important factor in my development [1999, p. 18].

The Parent Substitute

Children who strive to achieve the elite level in their area of talent spend a great deal of time with their instructors. It is very common for the child and the instructor to develop a special bond that often resembles the parent-child relationship. The biographies of top achievers are filled with fond remembrances of special mentors, coaches, and teachers who are recalled as being "part of my family." Many say, "He was just like a father to me," and "I could talk to my coach about anything, and she would understand and help me."

In some cases, instructors do fill a parental gap in dysfunctional families. This was the case for boxer Mike Tyson; Tyson lived several years in the household of his coach, Gus D'Amato, who eventually became Tyson's legal guardian when Tyson was seventeen. I myself have consulted on a case in which a gymnastics coach took a young girl under her wing and gave her the love and support that the child's emotionally distant parents had not been able to do. Throughout history, coaches, tutors, and instructors have often been parent surrogates. But this type of relationship is a cause of growing concern at this time, as youth programs often shift toward a more professional model with huge potential financial rewards, a shift that puts the motive of these parent substitutes clearly into question.

There are several problems that can develop when an instructor becomes a parent substitute. It can be a risk to the full development of a child if the instructor lacks knowledge of the child's needs outside the area of talent. Can a win-at-all-costs type of instructor recognize that a child star has other emotional, mental, and developmental needs outside the performance arena? If not, he can offer only one-dimensional parenting that will skew the child's view of life and of self.

A parent-substitute relationship usually develops in situations where the parents are initially glad that an instructor has taken a personal interest in their child. They notice that the instructor spends more time with their child than with other children. They are happy, even relieved, to allow him to take their child to social events, such as the movies or a concert. They assume that this interest will both help the child enjoy her lessons more and improve her chances of gaining opportunities to compete or excel over the instructor's other students. But soon the parents notice that the instructor is making decisions that might be unhealthy or inappropriate for their child.

Maria's figure skating instructor, for example, told her to skip school on Friday so she could get in more hours of practice before

A Very Needy Situation

An ABPD parent-substitute situation is especially likely to develop when the child or the coach is in a vulnerable emotional state. Children who come from homes where they are neglected or emotionally or physically abused are hungry for a close adult relationship and will look to their instructors for attention and support. At the same time, instructors who are experiencing emotional or social deprivation in their own lives are likely to breach the boundaries of their relationships with children and seek to be a loving and protective parent substitute.

her performance on Saturday. Hal's math tutor gave him a collection of herbal supplements to improve his brainpower. Kathleen's fencing coach registered her for a residential summer camp. All of these instructors made parental decisions without first gaining permission from the child's parents.

In cases like these, the instructors are doing what they think best for the child's progress in his or her area of talent—not what is best for the overall well-being of the child. This is the difference between an appropriately caring parent and an ABPD instructor. This is a situation that you must guard against. If your child's instructor begins to make parental decisions without your consent, don't hesitate to immediately insist that all decisions regarding your child's life be discussed with you first. Instructors who know that the parents are not going to hand over their children without question are less likely to take advantage of their power and are more likely to monitor their boundaries.

A Dancer's Dream

In some cases a parent-substitute relationship develops over the objections of the child's parents. In these cases, the child is at grave risk of suffering the consequences of ABPD behaviors. A recent example is the story of Misty Copeland, who many in the dance world

---

Accepting the Occasional Takeover

There are some instances when an instructor may safely take control from the parents. If your child's instructor tells you to back off, consider the circumstance. If it's an occasional request during particularly tense times when your presence may be distracting to your child or when it's important that the child doesn't receive conflicting instructions, it won't harm your child to let the coach be in charge. This usually happens during intense competitions and sometimes when traveling on the road. But when an instructor expects complete control all the time, it is time for you to exert your authority, even if this means taking the child and walking away.

feel was on the brink of stardom when her training was interrupted by a bitter feud between her mother and her dance teachers. That feud sparked an unusual legal battle over the control of the young dancer's future, played out in national headlines and on television talk shows.

At the age of twelve, Misty lived in a one-bedroom motel room with her mother, Sylvia Delacerna, and four of her six siblings. Misty's dreams of being a dancer with the American Ballet Theater began the day she met Cynthia Bradley at the Boys and Girls Club in San Pedro, California. Cynthia, who was the artistic director of a local ballet company, was there giving free dance classes to underprivileged children when she spied the raw talent in Misty.

Soon Misty began taking free classes at Bradley's private dance studio. But getting there meant spending two hours a day on the bus because her mother did not have a car. After several months, her mother worried that the long commute to the dance studio was taking a toll on Misty, and she told her daughter she would have to quit. That's when Cynthia offered to have Misty live with her Monday through Friday and go home on the weekends.

The deal was struck, and Misty moved in with Cynthia and her husband Patrick. Misty started homeschooling so that she could spend hours each day getting first-class training. The Bradleys supported her both financially and professionally. Misty told one reporter, "They became like family to me." And Cynthia has admitted that she came to consider Misty her daughter.

Misty blossomed and began to attract national attention. The teen prodigy was on her way to becoming a prima ballerina. But Sylvia Delacerna began to resent the people who made it possible. Misty began to skip her visits home on weekends, and Sylvia felt that the Bradleys were trying to steal Misty away from her. The tension and resentment mounted until Sylvia told her daughter that after two-and-a-half years of living with her teachers, she had to move back home and could no longer train with the Bradleys. This news pushed Misty to file for emancipation from her mother and give her the legal rights of an adult. She then went into hiding for three days, on the advice of the Bradleys.

Convinced that the Bradleys were behind her daughter's disappearance and were trying to take away her child, Sylvia filed court papers of her own, asking for a restraining order to keep the

Bradleys away from her daughter. The battle over Misty was now a public courtroom issue.

Eventually Misty dropped her quest for emancipation and moved back home. She returned to high school and enrolled in a local ballet school with a different teacher. But many in the dance world say that training after school with a local teacher is not intensive enough and that Sylvia's refusal to allow the Bradleys to intensively train Misty may cost her daughter her (and their) dream. But Sylvia insists, "The dance community can't decide what's best for Misty. I'm her mother. I'll decide what's best for her. I will make sure she's always into dance" ("Epic Battle for the Heart of a Child Prodigy," 1998).

Misty proved that her mother's decision did not kill her dreams: she won a scholarship to a summer program sponsored by the American Ballet Theater in New York City. There she was offered what some say was a once-in-a-lifetime opportunity: an invitation to join the company. But again, Misty's mom wanted her home to finish her senior year of high school and spend more time with her siblings. Misty is hoping the company will still want her when the year is over (Adato, 1999).

The question of who's right and who's wrong in this life drama is not easily answered. The story serves simply as a real-life illustration of the serious problems that can arise when instructors become parent substitutes.

The Sexual Abuser

Children who need specialized instruction spend a lot of time away from home in the company of their chaperoning instructors and other children's parents. Unfortunately this situation supplies a ready-made resource pool and environment for pedophiles. Anecdotal information on the number of children who are sexually molested by the person entrusted with their care tell a very alarming story that parents can't ignore. Although there have been no formal studies conducted to determine exactly how many child molesters are out there training our athletes, scholars, and performing artists, the numbers and cases we do have are staggering.

A recent article in *Sports Illustrated* reported that a computer database search of recent newspaper stories revealed more than thirty cases in just the previous eighteen months of coaches in the United States who had been arrested or convicted of sexually abusing children engaged in sports (this despite the fact that child victims of sexual abuse rarely report the crime) (Nack and Yaeger, 1999).

In most cases, parents have no idea what's going on. This certainly has been the case in Canadian junior ice hockey; kids often leave home at fourteen or fifteen and live with local families as powerful coaches lead them on their first steps toward an NHL career. In 1990, after his team won the national midget championship, Stephane Valois of Sorel, Quebec, was charged with three counts of sexual assault on minors and was sentenced to five months in jail. In 1991, former Drummondville (Quebec) coach Jean Begin was convicted of seven counts of sexual assault on boys; he committed suicide after serving a six-month prison sentence. In 1996, the Quebec Ice Hockey Federation barred Martin Dubuc from coaching after he was convicted of sexual assault on two players. (He later returned to coaching.) Most notable of all was the case in 1997 in which acclaimed junior coach Graham James pleaded guilty and was sentenced to three-and-a-half years in prison for the sexual assault of Sheldon Kennedy and another player who maintained anonymity. Kennedy, a winger with the Boston Bruins, claimed he was sexually assaulted more than 350 times over a ten-year period by James. "At fifteen in the hockey world, it's a tough thing to do, to say a man has touched you or made sexual moves on you," Kennedy said. "You don't want to wreck your dreams. There was absolutely nowhere for me to turn. I had no one, nobody" (Elliott, 1997, p. C8). How sad and calamitous that despite the frequency of instructor-child abuse, victims always feel alone and isolated.

Educators are also well represented as professionals guilty of sexual abuse of their students. Nearly 40 percent of the teaching licenses revoked by the California Commission of Teacher Credentialing in a recent one-year period were revoked for reasons of sexual misconduct (Romano, 1995). And a recent case in New Jersey highlights the problem among performing artists: a well-respected piano teacher was charged with fondling his female students (and videotaping the abuse) during their private lessons; he killed himself when the charges were made public.

It is well known that pedophiles can be doting parents, great teachers, and successful, well-loved instructors. At the same time, they are heinous, conscience-deficient predators, many themselves having suffered abuse early in life. Power and control through sexual gratification is often their chief motivation, but parts of their personality and behavior can also be attributed to ABPD. It is ABPD that leads these adults to expect or demand reward and privilege such as physical or sexual access from the objectified elite, young, naive individual in return for often-outstanding and time-consuming coaching, teaching, or mentoring. This is often enthusiastically supported by parents. The power differential inherent in instructive situations, the physical closeness involved in teaching and perfecting physical skills, and the long periods of time alone with elite, obedient children away from families allow domineering, charismatic, patient, devious, and unfortunately deviant individuals to sexually exploit children. In these cases, the instructor clearly has lost the ability to differentiate his own aberrant physical and psychological needs from a child's bodily integrity and boundaries. Such individuals often have highly developed rationalizing abilities to justify their criminal behavior.

A Position of Trust

A recent, very instructive and frightening case of sexual abuse by a trusted figure is one of Peter Fischer, a charismatic, bright California pediatrician who sexually molested his male HMO patients through at least two decades, despite complaints that went essentially unheeded. His position, power, intelligence, and charm, along with his concurrent financial and multidimensional compensatory nurturance of his victims and the refusal by colleagues, administrators, and parents to lend credence to the victims' complaints, all played their part in his criminal subterfuge. Of great concern, as well, is that as an excellent tennis player, he privately coached young players; his most notable pupil was international champion Pete Sampras, whom he coached (apparently for free!) from the time Sampras was eight until he was eighteen (Goldsmith, 1999). (Sampras has not as yet accused Fischer of molesting him.)

Five Major Mistakes

The following are the five biggest mistakes parents can make regarding the potential for sexual abuse:

1. Assuming that their child's trusted instructor would never sexually abuse their child.
2. Assuming that if their child is not complaining about a problem, there is none.
3. Not believing their child who even once reports correctly on clearly abusive behavior.
4. Not notifying other parents of children who have also had contact with this instructor. (Sexual predators are as a rule serial abusers over many years before they are apprehended.)
5. Assuming that informed, generally responsible organizations will appropriately discipline an abusive but often valuable member of their team.

Remember: instructors who sexually exploit children don't jump out of the bushes to attack. They spend a long time building up a relationship. They are often personable, charismatic, and well liked. They use their position to win over the parents so they can spend more unquestioned time with the children. They are invited over for dinner, they spend holidays together, they exchange birthday gifts, they become part of the family. Then with infinite patience and kindness they break down the children's inhibitions with flattery, attention, and affection until they are able to seduce and molest them. This scenario is played out every day within the full range of pedophilic sexual preferences. Some male instructors molest male children; others molest females. Some female instructors or teachers molest male children; others molest females. Often the abuse continues for years, and the parents are the last to know (if they ever know at all).

The following are some typical cases of sexual abuse:

A seventeen-year-old female honor student who had an "affair" with her forty-two-year-old English teacher throughout her senior year of high school. This teacher became a close friend of the family and was even entrusted with the care of the teenager when the parents went out of town for the weekend.

A twelve-year-old boy who was abused by his youth football team coach during Saturday night sleepovers. It was eventually discovered that the boy was sexually abused over a three-year period in the coach's downstairs rec room while his wife and two young daughters slept upstairs.

A seven-year-old female figure skater whose male instructor used the close physical contact of "spotting" (lifting and holding and supporting) to inappropriately fondle the child until she complained to her mother of soreness around her breasts and genital area.

A fourteen-year-old male pianist who "fell in love" with his twenty-year-old female instructor during his month-long stay at a summer residential music camp.

In all of these cases, and in the probable thousands of unreported cases that occur across the country every year, there is the risk of a dangerous violation of boundaries that victimize the children, leaving lasting emotional trauma associated with unremitting guilt, shame, and despair, and causing stress disorders as well as a diminished ability to trust and to develop normal, fulfilling relationships.

Prevention Is Key

Although the vast majority of instructors are certainly not sexual predators, the potential for sexual exploitation and boundary violation by an instructor is a very real possibility. The key to dealing with this possibility is prevention. The following guidelines, adapted from tips offered by the National Center for Missing and Exploited Children, will help you keep your child safe:

- Do a background check. Ask if your child's school, team, or class conducts a criminal history check or any other types of background checks on the instructors. If it does not, you can do it yourself and lobby with other parents for a change in this policy. Some states make their registry of sex offenders avail-

Not with My Kid

Parents are sometimes blinded to the dangers of sexual abuse if an athletic coach has a winning record and an engaging personality. In New Bedford, Massachusetts, for example, a successful youth basketball coach was forced out of the AAU after parents complained that he took whirlpool baths in the nude with their sons, requiring them to remove all their clothes before entering the hot tub. After the complaints were made, it was found that this coach had previously been convicted of "unnatural acts with children under sixteen" and then later convicted again for being "a lewd person in speech and behavior." The remarkable and disturbing feature of this case is that this person is still coaching with the support of parents who are aware of his past record!

In a similar case in New Jersey, a popular coach and gym teacher was accused of having sex with a teenager. During his trial, the judge received one hundred letters from supporters, despite the fact that it was now public knowledge that the defendant had previously served time for molesting a younger girl.

able on the Internet. Otherwise, a criminal check by police should cost no more than $40 per person.

- Don't turn your child's instructor into a baby-sitter. Studies show that men predisposed to molest children often gravitate to and prey first on those regularly left unattended by parents. Show you are actively involved in your child's life.

- Don't fall for flattery. Beware of instructors who gush with praise for your child's talents. They may be trying to win your trust and groom your child for seduction.

- Talk to your child at regular intervals throughout his or her childhood and then be able to listen in a positive and non-judgmental fashion. Describe for your son or daughter in detail what you consider inappropriate behavior by an instructor (improper touching of private body parts, prolonged nudity—certainly with supervising adults—showing pornographic material, offering alcohol or drugs). Assure your child that he or she will never get in trouble with you for telling the truth.

- Beware of instructors bearing excessive gifts. It is not normal behavior for a nonparent to shower a child with gifts. This is a warning sign that at the very least something unusual and possibly inappropriate is going on.
- Stay informed. Make sure you know where your child is, where the team is playing, where the performances are scheduled. Don't let an instructor keep you in the dark claiming confidentiality.

As the leader of the team that is supporting your child's talents, you must stay alert to the possibility of sexual abuse by your child's instructor. Following the aforementioned guidelines is a major step toward keeping your growing child happy, healthy, sane, and out in front.

ADVICE FROM THE EXPERTS

This chapter made it clear that it's important to really know the people we trust to mentor and coach our children. We asked three experts to tell us about their experiences with both nurturing and abusive adult-child relationships. These experts are (1) Fred Engh, founder and president of the National Alliance for Youth Sports, (2) Sally Reis, Ph.D., president of the National Association for Gifted Children, and (3) Deborah Mitchell, D.M.A., director of music education at the College of the Arts at California State University, Long Beach.

Athletics

Fred Engh is the founder and president of the National Alliance for Youth Sports, an organization dedicated to the training and certification of volunteer coaches. He has been involved in youth sports for over thirty years as coach, athletic director, and sports educator. We asked him to discuss coaching styles that are desirable and those that are dangerous.

"In 1984, I attended a conference on youth sports in which a pediatrician delivered a speech claiming that youth sports was 'the greatest form of legalized child abuse in America.' Like many in the audience that day, I sat there stunned. My initial reaction was, how could he make such a statement about something that had the wonderful ability to positively influence a child's life? Today, I realize he had a very good point. Sometimes, the coach's actions in search of the Almighty Win must be called child abuse. It may not be deliberate; it may amount to ignorance, indifference, or arrogance; but in any event, it puts at risk the safety of the children under his care.

"The notion that there's any other goal involved in youth sports coaching than to win never even dawns on many coaches. Their every action is guided by a single principle: What can I do to get my team a win? Forget about developing character, forget about providing a model of good sportsmanship, and forget about whether or not the children are actually having fun. The only thing that matters is having a winning team.

"This attitude teaches the kids life lessons as well. They learn that if it's OK to cheat in sports, it's OK to cheat in life. If injuring the opposing player is the only way I can win, then that's what I'll do. And if that's what it takes to get ahead at school or work, then I'm justified. Every child in whom we instill these attitudes is one more person we're sending out into the world who will contribute to the moral decay of our society.

"Children who are participating in organized sports don't deserve to be treated as miniature adults, to be pushed into competitive sports before they're ready, to be physically and emotionally abused, to suffer needless injuries, and to be pressured into sacrificing their childhood years for the sake of athletic excellence. It takes a lot of work to restore our youngsters' faith in working hard toward a goal when they are faced with negative experiences. Under the right conditions, many youth sports experiences can be enormously beneficial, teaching the importance of teamwork, cooperation, and hard work. But in

Work Until You Drop

Even those who "made it" aren't always in agreement with the training schedules they endured as children. An Olympic swimmer recalls,

> I went through a summer as a fourteen-year-old where I literally worked out in the pool three times a day, seven days a week. My coach said, "We're going to go on a horrendous workout schedule, but I think it will make you better." Well, you cannot throw a human being into a pool and work them until they drop dead. I was swimming nine or ten miles a day. I was just plumb worn out, mentally and physically. My coach lost sight of the fact that you're dealing with not only the physical attributes, but also the mental attributes. He never asked can this person withstand the mental strain of being torn down like this. After a while I just couldn't tolerate it anymore. I just lost confidence in my coach [Bloom, 1985, p. 162].

spite of this potential for good, many youth sports experiences, under the wrong conditions, can be emotionally damaging— and that damage can last a lifetime."

Academics

Sally M. Reis, Ph.D., is president of the National Association for Gifted Children and professor of educational psychology at the University of Connecticut. We asked Dr. Reis to describe what parents should look for in a teacher who works with very bright children.

"Good teachers have a passion for the subject and model a love of learning. Some instructors get so caught up with drilling facts, trying to meet standards, and getting scores up on the state mastery tests that they drain the enjoyment out of the learning process. These experiences can kill a child's ability to realize his or her full potential. Children have to cooperate in the learning process and make a conscious effort to use and develop their academic abilities, and if learning isn't enjoyable and exciting, this may not happen. It is essential that we don't always place bright students in accelerated programs that stress content over enjoyment in learning and discovery and the use of talents to pursue independent self-directed learning. Options for creativity and imagination are also necessary.

"I also believe that high-achieving children need teachers who value creative thought. But unfortunately, the focus on state testing, standardized learning, and core mastery skills may be drumming creativity out of our schools. This is a real problem because it's the absence of creative opportunities that so often turn bright students into underachievers by the end of their elementary school years. They are turned off by the textbook learning they find so easy and boring. Unfortunately, the strategy for dealing with underachievers is often to give them more, but higher-level, textbooks. When this doesn't spark any renewed interest in learning, some parents enroll them in out-of-school programs that again focus on content only, and the underachievement may continue.

"It's important to find teachers who think more about the individual student than the state assessment tests. There are fine teachers out there who can differentiate curriculum to meet individual needs. They also care about the unique interests of each child. They work with individual learning styles and explore children's interests. They take an enrichment approach to learning with exposure to libraries, museums, experiments, and the like. Parents should find teachers in their child's school who let kids do creative projects. Which ones challenge individual students to pursue personal interests? Which ones can create a balance between enjoyment and hard work? These are the teachers we want for all of our children."

Performing Arts

Deborah Mitchell, D.M.A., is director of music education at the College of the Arts at California State University, Long Beach. She also taught previously at the Colburn School in Los Angeles. We asked her to share her opinion about the traits and qualities of a good performing arts instructor.

"I have seen parents travel hours to give their children the opportunity to study with renown teachers. I know of a family

---

Summers of Learning

The book *Developing Talent in Young People* (Bloom, 1985) offers a glimpse at the upbringing of a selected group of American mathematicians who have reached the highest level of accomplishment and respect in the field. In one case study, the author shares a story that supports Dr. Reis's feeling that bright children have an opportunity to learn more when they're not in the classroom. In this case, young "Hal" spent every summer of his youth until he finished college visiting with his grandfather in a rural mountain setting. This grandfather had a Ph.D. in mathematics but spent most of his time with his grandson building things, having discussions, and going fishing and hiking. Despite this lack of structured learning, Hal recalls, "He was an excellent teacher. I think my grandfather did influence me a great deal in the direction of mathematics" (p. 339).

who flew their young daughter from California to Boston every other week to take her music lessons. Many parents will make great sacrifices in their own lives to give their children the best training possible. I think, however, that too many of these parents use an instructor's reputation for turning out 'stars' as their sole criterion when choosing an instructor. For children, this is not always all that matters.

"It's important to tune into your children to find out if a certain kind of training is the kind they need and want. High-achieving kids are usually mature enough around the age of nine or ten to have a say in how they study their art. If you are considering hiring a demanding teacher, you need to say to your child, 'This is going to require many hours of practice on your part. It's going to be a sacrifice on my part in terms of time and finances. I am willing to do anything for you if you really want this.' The likelihood of problems is reduced if the child is personally committed to the requirements of the instructor.

"Communication in general is very important when you want your child to get the most benefit from his or her lessons. Parents should listen to a child's complaints if the child and the instructor are not getting along. Some complaints simply vent personal frustrations. But if the instructor is pushing the child beyond a level he or she feels comfortable with, it's time for the parent to talk with the teacher. I realize that it is a very difficult line for the parent to walk between being too controlling and properly protective, but it helps if the lines of communication between child and parent and parent and instructor are always open. Good instructors make themselves available to talk with parents at times when the child isn't in earshot. They are open to talking about their goals for the child, the child's potential, the method of training, and so on.

"A good instructor also recognizes the importance of childhood and the peer culture. If the instructor feels, for example, that practicing for a recital is more important than going to a high school prom, then the parent has to step in and say, 'I want my child to have time for other things that are important to her.' Parents should not give up their decision-making authority to any instructor. They should stay involved with the lessons and be aware of the way they influence other areas of the child's life.

"I think the best instructors are the ones who not only have an exceptional knowledge of skill training, but who will also get to know the whole child. The instructor should care about what the child likes and dislikes. He or she should know the name of the family dog, for example, and should be able to develop a special rapport with each child. Even demanding teachers need to have warmth and caring attitudes. They should understand the stages of child development and have patience to see each child through difficult periods. The teachers that I learned the most from in my career were the ones who recognized that I was a person, not just another violinist.

"I would stay away from instructors who are focused too intently on competitions. Often these people live in the reflected glory of their students and place competition preparation over learning and improving. I've heard young pianists practicing Bach pieces for months and months for a competition that offers only the benefit of making the teacher look good. Children need time to grow, experiment, and take risks with their art. Too many competitions can be stifling.

"I'd also suggest that families stay away from a teacher who feels he or she is the only teacher the child will ever need. Although you don't want to move young children around too often because they can get too much conflicting information, older children can benefit from a change of instructors. Studying with many teachers gives a performer different insights, perspectives, and techniques. You want a teacher who is secure enough to say when it's necessary, 'I think you should move on to another teacher. I have taken you about as far as I can.'

"Parents should definitely interview a prospective teacher by asking for a sample lesson. Some teachers give these for free; others charge a fee. But either way, it's an excellent way to get a feel for the kind of instructor you're going to hire. Of course, you expect the instructor to have a certain level of skill, but there are other things you should look for as well. In this environment you can get an idea of the way the teacher interacts with students. You'll notice if the teacher asks the child personal questions about things like school or hobbies (which is an indicator that the teacher sees children as people rather than just students). You'll see the teaching style and the materials used.

You can get an idea about the person's sense of compassion and ethical standards. Before making any kind of commitment, this arrangement gives your child an opportunity to get a feel for this person and have a say in how he or she feels about working with her.

"Children in the performing arts spend a lot of time with their teachers. It's worth the effort to make sure the child and the instructor are a good match."

Never Exploited, Battered, or Abused

Instructors who bully, dominate, and molest have made a home for themselves in the worlds of athletics, academics, and the performing arts. But if you are not in an ABPD trap yourself, you will recognize when your child is being exploited, battered, or abused and will take quick steps to find a new instructor (even if that means risking your child's opportunity to be a star). If you stay in charge of your child's training, you will find instructors who support, guide, nurture, and help children reach their full potential both as high achievers and as human beings.

Once you are assured that your child's instructor is not working from an ABPD position, you can then move on to weighing the value versus the cost of the sacrifices and commitment required at the top. Step Four will show you how.

Step Four

Weigh the Cost of Sacrifice

Raising a high-achieving child is often a family or village affair in which everyone makes sacrifices to nurture the talented child. Usually, the child herself will sacrifice the time required to practice or study. The parents will sacrifice their time to chauffeur their child to practices and events, and their money to buy necessary equipment and often to travel to distant instructors and competitions. Even siblings sacrifice their time to accompany the family to games, performances, special events, and practices. There is nothing objectionable about these sacrifices, but there is a wide gulf between normal family sacrifices and sacrifices made by families caught in Achievement by Proxy Distortion (ABPD) traps.

The normal range of supportive Achievement by Proxy (ABP) behavior includes an element of "normal" sacrifice. Parents are able to, desire to, and indeed are expected to make reasonable sacrifices for their children within the cultural context of their lives. In return, the children morally "owe" their parents something: they owe reciprocal responsible behavior, respect, and effort. Children whose parents take them to Saturday classes at a distant university have an obligation to complete their assignments to the best of their ability. Children whose parents pay the fees and shuttle their kids back and forth to the "best" coaches and sport teams have the obligation to give the sport their best effort. Children who take music lessons have a responsibility to practice.

Parents may also require sacrifices that ensure a child's ability to continue developing in her area of talent. A dancer, for example, remembers being forbidden to go skiing with her friends for fear a broken leg would set back her training. A college baseball player recalls having to sit out the whiffle ball games his friends played in elementary school because his dad felt that playing with the light-weight bat and ball would throw off his bat speed. And a pianist re-calls that her mother told the softball coach she could no longer play the coveted position of catcher because she might break a fin-ger. In these cases, the required sacrifices were both supportive and not unreasonable, even though they were annoying to the child at the time and may have contributed to a sense of social isolation and unidimensionality.

Most parents and their high-achieving children realize that as-piring to a place on an Olympic team, going for a full college schol-arship, or hoping for a seat in the New York Philharmonic requires incredible commitment and time in preparation, by both the child and parent. However, there is always a serious risk of ABPD when parents and children make risky sacrifices to reach these goals that require some kind of long-term payback in order to be considered worthwhile.

I have counseled many parents who have made risky sacrifices that apply increasing pressure on their children to be high achiev-ers. As we have discussed elsewhere, some parents take on a sec-ond or even a third job solely to support a child's pursuits. Some families move great distances, uprooting their entire household, in order to be closer to a training facility; others allow a child to live at a training facility or even to be adopted into the custody of a coach or instructor. I have met parents who have changed jobs or reconfigured their work lives to have more time to dedicate to the child. Some have taken the drastic step of quitting their own jobs to devote themselves entirely to their child's career as man-ager or coach or both.

Once the family makes these kinds of major sacrifices, the child is often expected to reciprocate with equally colossal, risky sacrifices of her own. She may be required to practice eight hours a day. She may be expected to maintain or lower her weight. A child's normal social life may be prohibited or indefinitely delayed in order to focus on a training regimen. Some children are expected to sacrifice a quality general education for hit-or-miss homeschooling or tutoring so they have more time to dedicate to the development of their talent. Some sacrifice their health to stress-related ailments or physical injuries, and many sacrifice their short- and long-term emotional and psychological well-being to overbearing, controlling, and sometimes abusive instructors. (See Step Three for more information about abusive instructors.) The decision to make these sacrifices is often made with the best interest of the child at heart. But in truth they are risky sacrifices that can carry hefty monetary, emotional, and physical price tags.

In this chapter we take a look at some of the common sacrifices families and children make in their quest to be the best, and we will ask you to weigh the cost of those sacrifices against their benefits. Sometimes the cost-benefit scale will be in balance or will favor the benefits; at other times it will be a clear negative mismatch, when one looks at it both in the present and with the benefit of hindsight.

Childhood Sacrifices

Do you think it would it be worth it for your child to give up a "normal" childhood to practice seven hours a day for four years for the *possibility* of earning a place on an Olympic team and *possibly* earning a gold medal and *possibly* gaining millions of dollars in endorsements and engagements? Your honest answer to this question will give you an idea of where you stand on the issue of childhood sacrifices. Some people believe that no sacrifice is too great when it comes to making dreams come true. Others hesitate to disrupt what most consider a normal childhood.

Looking Back for Tara Lipinski

The life of Olympic skater Tara Lipinski glorifies the kinds of sacrifices some families make for their high-achieving children. At the age of ten, Tara and her mother moved from their home in Sugar Land, Texas, to suburban Detroit so Tara could train six days a week with her skating coach Richard Callaghan (still under a cloud of sexual molestation charges). Her father stayed behind to earn the money to pay the bills for the coach, the choreographer, the condo, the costumes, and the competitions. He became a financial lifeline and a weekend visitor in the life of his only child. Tara's mother also willingly sacrificed her comfortable marital life by moving with Tara and supervising her training. Tara sacrificed too in the short term. She gave up her friends and her dad, and the right to play other sports, join school activities, and hang out at the mall. But in the end, when Tara became the youngest individual gold medalist in any winter Olympics, the entire family agreed that it was worth every bit of sacrifice.

But how would the Lipinskis feel if Tara had not made the Olympic team (as so many thousands of young girls who sacrifice their childhood do not)? When weighing the cost of sacrifices, it's enlightening to do so from the point of view of relative failure. Given the sacrifices she made, if Tara did not make the Olympic team or did not win a medal, would she still be able to enter adulthood physically, emotionally, and mentally intact? Would her family survive the disappointment and still view Tara as a worthwhile person? Would Tara feel, at age sixteen, that her life had been wasted? There are no definitive answers to these questions, but asking them and using the guidelines set out in this book should help make you think twice and even three times before allowing your child to sacrifice big chunks of childhood (or demanding that he do so) to an often unattainable dream.

Teen Sacrifices

A sacrifice of teenage social time is very common among those who have achieved great things. The renowned violinist Isaac Stern recalls, "In those years, there was at least for me, no 'dating,' as the term is understood today. I remember a girl coming to me one day in a diaphanous dress and asking me to 'listen to her play.' I listened, and that was it. I didn't know what else to do. My teenage life was music" (1999, p. 21).

When judging the value of a sacrifice, try to look at the long-term picture and decide if you would still support your child's sacrifices if your child does not come out on top in five or ten years. Ask yourself:

Will my child gain something valuable even if he does not rise above the rest? Is it good enough if he walks away from this experience having learned the value of persistence, competition, travel, and new friends?

If my child's dream changes, will this still have been a valuable experience, and will her sacrifices have been worthwhile because of what she has learned about herself and her potential?

Does the sacrifice bring my child something of value in the present, such as a willingness to exert personal effort to achieve personal gain?

Putting your own real hopes and dreams aside, evaluate the sacrifices your child is making to attain high-level achievement. If you honestly feel that his sacrifices have value of their own—regardless of the outcome—then the sacrifices your child makes to attain these things may not be part of the objectification and possible abuse that defines families afflicted by ABPD.

I wonder how the parents of Fred An from Washington state feel about their son's sacrifice now as they look back on it. Since his

Enjoying the Trip Along the Way

"If your goals are too narrow, too high, too focused, too soon, it's a prescription for trouble in the long run. If you don't make it all the way to your goal, you still have two-thirds of your life left to live, so you'd better enjoy the *process*. If it takes four thousand steps to get to the Olympics but you only make three thousand of them, this is not a failure; you've come a long way and learned many things."

Dave Feigley, sports psychologist and chair of the
Department of Exercise Science and Sports Studies
at Rutgers University

childhood, the Ans wanted their son to attend the University of California at Berkeley. To improve his chances of going to Berkeley as a California resident, Fred moved away from his family, his friends, and his school to live in a condo by himself at the age of fifteen near the Berkeley campus. "Ever since eighth grade," remembers Fred, "my parents wanted me to move down to California. It was a hard decision for both of us." At his new high school, Fred earned a 3.5 grade point average and an SAT score of 1150—both far below the Berkeley average. Sadly, Fred was not accepted into the college of his dreams; instead, he went to another college where his life goes on—without fond memories of high school days spent with his family and friends ("Secrets of the SAT," 1999). Was his sacrifice worth it? Only Fred and his family can answer that for themselves. One hopes that the autonomy and independence skills Fred gained, and the ongoing closeness of his family, made up for the distance, disappointment, and financial and emotional hardship of this period of his adolescence.

Separating Talent from Identity

Ours is definitely an age of early specialization. Younger and younger children are asked to sacrifice the joy of "fun" activities to focus more seriously on their one area of talent. It's now unusual to find a blue-chip athlete who letters in three varsity sports. It is uncommon to find exceptional dancers, gymnasts, or skaters graduating at the top of their class, although Michelle Kwan is a good example. It is rare for a young computer whiz to enroll in a summer art program. To be the best at any one thing takes an inordinate amount of time, often leaving little room for anything else.

This may be a fact of our times for high-achieving children, but it should not require them to sacrifice their inborn identity as multidimensional people. As parents we do not raise a dancer or a scholar or an athlete; we must raise human beings who can grow into adulthood able to make mature decisions about what they want to do with their lives. We must raise individuals who have options so that their lives can be productive and joyful whether they reach the gold ring they are striving for or not.

The people who have the most trouble adjusting to "failure" or disappointment in life are those who define themselves by only one trait. In sports and performing arts this is particularly dangerous because even a professional who has "made it" will still desire to live an active and valued life when he loses the physical edge and must retire. This might explain the results of a research study conducted at the Olympic Training Center that asked successful athletes the question, "If you had a five-year-old child, what would you do in their upbringing, related to sports, the same or differently from your own upbringing?" More than half the athletes said that they would make sure that their child participated in other activities besides sports (Murphy, 1999).

The one-dimensional scholar, too, may not reach his goals because of his lack of depth. Yale University professor Robert Sternberg ("Secrets of the SAT," 1999) has cautioned applicants that high test scores are not the only criteria for admission to prestigious universities. "You'll find that many people are accepted who don't have the high SATs," he says, "but they have some degree of distinction in something else, because the competitive colleges don't want just a bunch of people who are good at getting A's; they want diversity. And so, you're actually doing your kids a favor if you help them develop other skills, not only for their success in life, but for giving them something that will distinguish them from other kids whose academic records and tests scores may be fine but who don't have anything else that sets them off."

The world is full of people who grew up as unidimensional children and have become dissatisfied, unhappy adults. We all know people like Paul, Andre, and Patricia: Paul is a forty-year-old computer programmer who spent his high school and college years training to be a professional vocalist. Andre is a thirty-five-year-old teacher who spent every summer of his youth at a camp in Canada practicing ice hockey. And Patricia is a fifty-year-old accountant who expected to become a college physics professor. Unfortunately, none of these people were ever encouraged to develop other interests along with their special talents. Because their sense of self-worth was very early on linked with accomplishment in one specific area in which they no longer excel, they now live their days in regret and with feelings of failure and internalized parental disappointment.

Fortunately, this sacrifice of self-worth is not inevitable. Multidimensional people have a kind of self-image insurance policy. Their identity is not formed only by what they can achieve. Consequently they have a well-grounded, nonfragile sense of self constructed on solid, supportive relationships from infancy. If they don't make it in one area, they have many other things to hold on to.

When your child is training to develop a certain skill, do him a favor that he will treasure for the rest of his life. Ask yourself this question: Am I both allowing and encouraging my child to grow and develop in other areas as well, to be a multidimensional person who has interests and resources that can cushion the dramatic fall from the top in the one area of talent?

Make a conscious effort to help your child explore *all* parts of her personality and abilities. Your child may feel confident in her athletic, academic, or performing arts skills, but she needs time and space to find other areas of interest as well. Take your young athlete to art museums and theatrical plays. Give your performing artist the tools he needs to explore the stars and the sea. Enroll your scholar

Versatile Prodigies

Some versatile prodigies have managed to combine other interests and attainments with their unusual musical talent (Fisher, 1973):

Violinist Charles Castleman made his successful debut recital at the age of ten. His extraordinary intelligence, coupled with an excellent general education, allowed him to appear at the same time with great success as a "Quiz Kid" on radio, in competition with some of the best young minds of the day.

Pianist Walter Gieseking was an ardent entomologist. He once stopped playing in the middle of an outdoor concert when a rare moth flew by, and did not resume his playing until he had caught it!

Violinist Fritz Kreisler not only became an accomplished pianist and painter but also was also a linguist and book collector, a student of medicine and an army officer. He once spoke of a favorite daydream: "In those youthful days I had some very weird thoughts about my future career. I envisioned myself operating on a patient in the morning, playing chess in the afternoon, giving a concert in the evening, and winning a battle at midnight" (pp. 183, 184).

in a martial arts or swimming class. Allow time for daydreaming and reading. When selecting library books, steer your child to new topics. Introduce your child to the whole world—the one that exists beyond her narrow area of exceptional talent.

In order to grow as a multidimensional person and avoid the hazards of ABPD, high-achieving children need to know that your love and support is not dependent on their accomplishments. You can convey this message by following these few simple guidelines:

- Give your children the freedom to take risks and make mistakes when trying new things, without risking your disappointment. (Remember, even unexpressed disappointment registers clearly with intuitive children.)
- Let them try things just for fun—even if they are impractical or have no market value or are of no personal interest to you.
- Tell them over and over again that they don't have to be the best at everything they do; explain that you're proud of them for trying new things and having a variety of interests.
- Don't make everything a competition. Let your young athlete enjoy his artwork without entering it in the local art show. Let your budding scholar participate in sports without worrying about being an all-star.
- Show as much interest in your child's "secondary" activities as you do in those in her area of special talent. If you wouldn't miss your super athlete's tennis match, don't miss his school play either.
- Don't overschedule your child's day. Giving her time to hang out and just daydream tells her that she is loved even when she isn't "achieving."
- Be multidimensional yourself. Role model for your children that acceptance of yourself does not depend solely on the achievement of a narrowly focused goal. Life is also about enjoying lots of different things.

Parental Sacrifices

We all sacrifice in untold, uncountable ways for the well-being of our children. We give them our time, our energy, our money, our love, and a large chunk of our lives. Indeed, parents of most mammalian species seem to be hard-wired through biological evolution to sacrifice for the betterment of their offspring. But sacrificing for the good of your child is quite different from sacrificing for your own personal gain based on the achievements of your child.

This section will help you stand back and look at the sacrifices you're making for the development of your child's talent, and then assess their true source. If your willingness to sacrifice is born primarily out of an altruistic, unselfish, and sincere desire to help your child reach his full potential, then your relationship with your child is on firm ground and will flourish regardless of how his talent shapes his future. Our motives, of course, need not eliminate pride and reflected glory, as they are normal as a dividend of our children's success. But if your sacrifices are rooted in your own frustrated dreams, missed opportunities, vicarious ambitions, or desire for financial gain or personal prestige, you are up to your eyeballs in an ABPD situation. In this case you can expect a parent-child relationship fraught with tension, anger, guilt, and unhappiness for many years to come.

Sacrifices of Career and Money

The most common parental sacrifices that easily become risky sacrifices center on career and finances. Because it often takes much time and money to give high-achieving children the tools, lessons, and support needed to develop, their parents are always putting their hand in their pockets while "schlepping" from one place to another. But what if parents do this expecting (consciously or not) a major payback that doesn't materialize?

What if a parent turns down a job promotion because the extra hours would cause him to miss his daughter's volleyball games? How will he feel if two years later she is sitting on the bench or playing poorly or, worse, not playing at all? What if a boy's parents spend thousands and thousands of dollars on computer camps and home equipment and software to keep him on the cutting edge of the evolving technology? How will they feel when their son suddenly "throws it all away" and becomes interested in literature and announces he is entering college as an English major?

The answers to these kinds of questions depend on the parents' motives for making the career and financial sacrifices for their child. If the athlete's father made his decision to turn down a promotion because showing support for his daughter was more important to him than the career opportunity, he will achieve that goal by being there for her whether she is the star or not. He and his daughter will both be glad the sacrifice was made, regardless of her future in volleyball, and they will have a strong relationship. But if this dad sacrificed his career because he needed the personal feeling of accomplishment he gained from her successes or because he calculated that she could earn a college scholarship that would offset the financial loss of turning down the promotion, he will undoubtedly feel let down and angry if she does not play in the spotlight. In addition, his daughter will feel guilty and ashamed that Dad is so clearly disappointed. A parent's motive makes all the difference!

Likewise, the value of the financial sacrifices made by the parents of the young scholar will depend on their reasons for channeling money into computer education. Did they offer those opportunities because he enjoyed it at that moment and they believed that computer training would be a valuable skill for everyone in the twenty-first century? Or did they do it only because they had their hearts set on making their son a computer engineer? Investing money in a child's dream is always risky if you don't acknowledge and accept the very real possibility that the child may change his dream and his goals. Long-term, tangible demands should not be contingent.

Sacrifice of Self

There is one other sacrifice that is likely to lead parents into an ABPD relationship with their children: the sacrifice of self. It is a common distortion of positive and noble nurturing to sacrifice your own identity and personal life to the accomplishments of your child.

Parents who willingly and selflessly put the development of their child's talents above all else—above their spouses, friends, and personal interests—run the risk of devaluing and objectifying themselves. They may live and breathe only for the achievements their children bring to them. Indeed, they run the risk of becoming, in a role-reversed fashion, emotionally and psychologically symbiotic with and dependent on their children.

Take the case of Marian, for example. Marian's daughter, Talya, wanted to be an actress. Throughout Talya's elementary school years, Marian accompanied Talya to see scores of Broadway plays. She coached her daughter through singing and dancing lessons. She scouted stage papers for open auditions. She attended all the rehearsals and performances of Talya's school and community plays. She made costumes, sold tickets, and rehearsed lines. She became friendly with other "stage" mothers. Her life was hectic, full, and very happy.

Then in her sophomore year of high school, the increasingly independent-minded Talya changed her plans. She said she was tired of "all that acting stuff," and she really didn't want to pal around with her mother any more. She turned down all Marian's invitations to go to plays or auditions. She stopped going to her voice teacher, and although she continued her dance lessons, she asked her mother to stop coming to each rehearsal with her. Instead of performing in plays, Talya got a job at a local clothing store and spent her free time hanging out with her friends. Talya seemed to have no regrets about her loss of interest in acting; other things interested her now. Her mother, however, did not adjust as well.

Without Talya's theatrical activities through which she had defined herself, Marian had nothing to do. Her friends were all involved in children's theater. She had no hobbies of her own. She had no interests outside of Talya. And because she and Talya had become such an inseparable twosome over the years, even her husband had stopped trying to gain her attention and time. With nothing to fill her days or her thoughts, Marian sank into a clinically severe major depression. She blamed Talya for cutting her out of her life. She blamed her husband for not caring that Talya was throwing away her talent. And she spent her days volleying between crying jags and angry outbursts.

Marian's ABPD level of risky sacrifice was severe, but not uncommonly so. Parents who inordinately focus their own lives toward sacrificing for their children often end up feeling betrayed and unhappy when independent children go their own way. In other families, obedient children can end up hopelessly unhappy when they continue in a sport or career that they have little interest in, and even despise, because they fear displeasing or disappointing their parents. Either way, the parent-child relationship is distorted.

To avoid this ABPD trap, you must make sure that your life has value of its own apart from your child's talent. Imagine your life if your child were to tell you today that she doesn't want anything more to do with her area of talent. Do you still have a life? Do you have friends? Hobbies? Plans? An honest evaluation of your own life, of your own ambitions and goals separate from your child's, will help you see if ABPD has wormed its way into your relationship with your child.

Self-Assessment

Before you sacrifice any more of your money, time, or self, double-check the boundary between your own desires and those of your child, always keeping in mind that ABPD muddies that line. Ask yourself:

Will this sacrifice be worth it if my child does not reach the top?

Am I certain it is my child's dream and not my own I am sacrificing for?

Do I expect my child to give me any kind of return on my investment, other than pride and satisfaction?

Am I willing to sacrifice my own life to make my child's dream come true? Why?

Have I let my child's goals replace my own?

Would I be willing to make these sacrifices if my child's talent were in a field in which I had no interest?

Without confronting questions like these, parents can get so caught up in the cost-benefit ratio of the sacrifices they are making for their child that they lose sight of the child. What if this "product" they have dedicated their lives to doesn't make it in the competitive marketplace? Or even worse, what if this product decides she doesn't want to compete in the marketplace anymore? How will the parents feel about their investment then? The belief that children owe their parents something in return for their sacrifices opens wide the door to ABPD objectification and abuse.

Parents' Sacrifice and the Value of Ambition

Nobel Prize winner Richard Feynman left his mark on virtually every area of modern physics. In his biography (Gleick, 1992), we learn that the senior Feynmans raised their children according to a silent creed shared with many of their neighbors: a parent does all he or she can to bring a child up, according to Richard's father, "so that he can better face the world and meet the intense competition of others for existence" (p. 28). With this idea in mind, the family tolerated and encouraged young Richard's experiments. If his mother's bridge partners asked how she could tolerate the noise, or the chemical smoke, or the not-so-invisible ink on the good linen hand towels, she said calmly that it was worth it. There were no second thoughts in the middle-class Jewish families of New York about the value of ambition on the children's behalf. They believed that "for the sacrifices of his parents a child owes no debt" (p. 28).

Sibling Sacrifices

If you are the parent of a high-achieving child who has siblings, we know what's on your wish list. You would like to be able to be in two (or three or four) places at one time. You would like a second or third set of hands, and you'd love to have forty-eight hours in every day. For many reasons, the parents of an exceptionally talented child often have more trouble than most spending equitable time with all their children. After all, supporting and encouraging the exceptionally talented child often means making that child's schedule a high priority in the family. The child's lessons, practice, and competitions in the field can easily dominate the family's routine. Family vacations, weekends, and social activities could become increasingly centered around this child, with the majority of time outside of school or jobs being spent in field-related pursuits.

The activities of the other children in the family pale in comparison. They don't get as much of the family time, attention, or resources because they aren't "elite" or intensive—they are just for fun. Without anyone realizing it, over time the high-achieving child begins to get special treatment. There are no pronouncements—"Because Josie is so talented everyone else in this family is going to have to take a back seat"—but every member of the family is aware of the attitude. This is not to say that requiring siblings to make some sacrifices to support their high-achieving brother or sister is necessarily an evil thing—it's just part of the package of being born into that family. It is how the parents handle the inequities that determines if they are struggling with an ABPD trap and jeopardizing the psychological health of all their children.

"Cinderella" Sacrifices

How easily the sibling of a high-achieving child can turn into a Cinderella. In many families, while the talented child "works" on his grueling and time-consuming study or practice, the siblings are asked to do the everyday chores of the household. This arrangement will seem reasonable or unfair depending on your viewpoint. *From a sibling's viewpoint:* if you ask young family members how they feel about the way their high-achieving siblings are treated, they're quick to point out the inequities they see:

"My parents never seemed to understand why I would complain about having to do the dishes or sweep the floors while my sister played piano. They would say, 'Your sister works on the piano; that is her job.' This seemed very fair to them."

"My brother was a swimmer, and he had to leave the house at five every morning. At seven o'clock my mother would make his bed, wake me, and remind me to make my own bed before I came downstairs. This seemed so unfair to me, and I started every day being furious at my brother, who from my point of view had it so easy."

"If my sister wasn't in school, she was at the roller skating rink, so she was never around when the garage needed to be swept or the car needed to be washed. I don't think my parents meant to treat me like a servant, but compared to my sister, who did no chores at all, that's how I felt."

As an adult, you know that one of the values of assigning children home chores is to teach them responsibility and self-discipline. You also realize that the high-achieving child can gain these traits many times over through the rigors of study and practice. It is easy to understand why you might not insist that your talented child put what little personal time he has into doing household chores. But keep in mind that this is a perspective that siblings do not share, and they may well be right. Even the "favored" child will feel guilty if her brother or sister is carrying an unfair load.

If equitable distribution of chores is a sore issue in your household, sit down with your children and talk. Map out what needs to be done and the amount of time each child has to contribute. Explain to siblings the amount of work and effort needed to develop an extraordinary talent. Explain to the talented child the work time needed to run the household. Ask the children to help devise a fair distribution of effort. If a sibling does the dinner dishes alone on the nights when his sister runs off to dance class, for example, maybe the dancer can vacuum her brother's bedroom on the weekends. You'll find that when siblings can help define their own "fair" regimen for doing chores, there is much less resentment. Also, children are bound to feel less "used" when you acknowledge their feelings and their point of view. The issue is not really doing the dishes per se, but rather the feeling that only the talented child gets parental time, attention, love, and admiration.

Attention Sacrifices

One parent can be in only one place at one time. This fact is bound to cause siblings of a high achiever to feel slighted on the family priority list. What's a parent to do when one child is competing in a national championship event on the same day and time as another child is competing in a hometown spelling bee? Either choice makes one child feel slighted, so it's not a matter of making everyone happy all the time—that's impossible. The sibling sacrifice of a parent's attention is damaging only when it is chronic and when the child learns that she is less valuable in her parent's eyes because her accomplishments are less spectacular.

Consider the family who has a twelve-year-old boy who is exceptionally talented in the martial arts. He trains five days a week at a facility twenty-five miles from his home, and he competes in local, regional, and national meets throughout the year. This family also has a nine-year-old girl who plays softball for her town team and plays the flute in her school band. The daughter knows that her brother's success is very important to her father because he had also trained in the martial arts as a young man and saw great value in this skill and discipline. This dad brings his son to every practice and stays to watch his progress. He attends every meet and takes off work when overnight travel is involved. This takes up all his free time, so he feels it goes without saying that he couldn't possibly also attend his daughter's games or concerts. Besides, father rationalizes that her mother supports her, and her activities are only for fun anyway—not as important as her brother's.

This scenario is not at all unusual. Siblings of exceptional children quietly learn, often with hidden resentments, to accept their position as less "important." (Take a look at the excellent book and film *Hillary and Jackie*.) But this doesn't have to be the norm. In your household you can make sure that although all your children may have to make some sacrifices to support the efforts of the high-achieving child, no one sacrifices a sense of self-worth or value.

The father in the foregoing anecdote feels justified devoting all his free time and attention to his son because he doesn't realize that this "attention" may in fact be an obsession rooted in ABPD. He needs to ask himself why it is that he can't miss his son's practice to attend some of his daughter's activities. Why is it that he thinks his son's interests have more value than his daughter's? It's quite likely that this father, and many parents like him, have made the dreams and goals of their "special" child their own. This is when they cross the line between the normal sense of accomplishment gained from a child's achievements and the distorted need to have the child fulfill the parents' own psychological needs.

Budgeting time among children is never easy in any family; it's always a juggling act that requires the wisdom of Solomon and sometimes his knife. But it can be done in a way that allows all the children to feel appreciated and valued. If you find yourself saying something like, "You know I'm proud of you, but I just can't be at your recital today because your brother is playing in a game that's really important," you've got some work to do. Telling your children you love them means nothing if your actions show that you're partial to one child and especially to his achievements. Sometimes you have to put your own wishes and desires on hold to do things with all your children to show that you love them for who they are, not for what they do.

Vacation Time

If the high achiever must spend time in a distant city to compete, train, or study, often the family will parlay these trips (which easily deplete the parents' allowed vacation days and financial resources) into some kind of vacation for the whole gang. This works out great if the trip brings the family to a resort area like Orlando, Florida, where there's plenty for everyone to do at Disney World. But the sacrifice becomes much greater when the "vacation" is spent in a place like Chickasha, Oklahoma—where many families spent their summer vacation of 1999 watching their sons compete in the AAU National Baseball Championship games. I'm sure there were many siblings at those games who were praying that when they returned to school they would not be assigned the customary essay on what they did on their summer vacation. From a sibling's point of view, spending seven days sitting in the 107 degree heat of the Midwest watching their brothers play baseball was not something to crow about.

This situation can be difficult to resolve. There are only so many vacation days and so much money available for family togetherness; it's not always as simple as spending some time on the road with your high achiever and some time at family-fun vacation spots. If you simply can't do both, it's time for a family meeting to explain the situation. If siblings have no choice in the matter, lay down the facts and then look for ways to ease the blow. Contact the city's division of tourism or chamber of commerce and find out where the amusement and water parks are located. Find the nearest lake or shore for family swimming, picnics, and boating. Reserve rooms in a hotel with a swimming pool, video arcade, sports facilities, and the like. In other words, don't get so wrapped up in one child's needs that you forget about the vacation needs of the rest.

One mother of an ice hockey star remembers spending a long winter weekend "vacation" in a small factory town in Massachusetts watching her son compete in an East Coast tournament. Her ten-year-old daughter was not at all happy. "This was not a place anyone would choose for a vacation," remembers this mom, "but in the end, it turned out to be a very memorable and special time for all of us. We found the area was full of antique shops, and my daughter and I spent a lot of time searching little shops for miniature tea sets and old hairpins and broaches. She still treasures the pieces we bought. I also decided to miss one of my son's games so my daughter and I could hop the train into Boston and spend half a day together doing lots of tourist-type stuff. There were other team parents who couldn't believe I would miss a game, but my son understood that his sister really needed time to do something that would make the trip enjoyable for her too. Today, I'm sure that my son doesn't even remember that I missed a game, but I know my daughter remembers every detail of her trip into Boston."

It's important to try to balance your attention even when the prime reason for the trip is to support one child's interests. When you have to travel to away events with the whole family, make sure that everyone has something to look forward to during the trip and that each one brings home memories of some fun time spent together.

On the Move

When a child shows exceptional promise in a particular area, she often needs specialized instruction. Unfortunately, the opportunity for this instruction may not be available in the area in which the family lives. In this case, it is not unusual for the whole family to move to a place where the talented child can have exposure to the best. Talented young musicians may need to move closer to large cities that have precollege training programs and notable youth orchestras. Young golfers may need to live in a warmer climate where there are more challenging courses and youth programs. Precocious scholars may need the stimulation of university classes that are open to children. For the benefit of the special child, the entire family sometimes packs up and moves.

When a major move is necessary, a parent caught in an ABPD trap will focus so intently on the needs of the talented child that she will expect the other children to go along without complaint. But if you ignore the needs and the feelings of the siblings during such a major life change, you can expect resentment and anger to grow. That's not saying you should cancel the move if a sibling complains, but it does mean that everyone's feelings have to be voiced and discussed. Moving to benefit the development of one child's talent is a major sacrifice for the entire family and certainly for the siblings—acknowledge that fact. Then find some way to make the move advantageous for everyone. Put time and energy into finding out what the new location offers the siblings. Give them something to get excited about: an interesting school program, a special room of their own in the new house, or the promise to have a close friend visit during the next school holiday. Don't let ABPD turn your other children into second-class family members whose feelings, needs, fears, and concerns are notably secondary to those of the high-achieving child.

Balancing a Sibling's Sacrifice

You can ease the burden of being the sibling of a high-achieving child by remembering these four tips:

1. Find a talent or interest within the sibling that does not compete with the "star." If your exceptional child is a gifted skier, encourage your other children to try other sports, such as swimming or tennis. Of course it's nice to have the whole family on the slopes together, but all the children don't have to compete in Kennedy-esque fashion. It's risky to let siblings fight for attention and praise in the same area. If one child's accomplishments continually fall short of the high mark already set by the high achiever, that child may soon decide he is a failure. Let him find his own area in which to excel.

2. Make a big deal of everyone's special moments: make every child in your family feel special and cherished. The high-achieving child often has news headlines and trophies to commemorate his accomplishments. So be sure to give something notable to all your children when they achieve a goal. Have balloons and a cake ready when your daughter makes the honor roll at school. Take pictures and videos and keep scrapbooks of other children's activities also.

3. Plan one-on-one activities. It's true that high-achieving children take up lots of our time, but parents caught up in ABPD frenzy use that as an excuse to focus solely on the needs of the talented child. Remember: having your other child standing next to you while you watch the talented child is not necessarily a quality-time experience. Make time if possible for all your children in activities where they can have your undivided attention. Take your other children out of the peanut gallery and put them in the spotlight of your attention as often as possible.

4. Be honest with yourself. It's easy to say, "I love all my children equally." It's much harder to show it. Ask yourself the following questions and answer them honestly. If you don't like your answers, do something about it by developing a real relationship with all your children:

Do the prime resources, encouragement, support, and instructional opportunities go to only one child?

Is there a gender bias in your preference to spend time with one child over another?

Are the sibling's achievements considered secondary to those of the most talented one (a la Joseph and his biblical brothers)?

Do you share in the dreams of all your children? Can you even name their dreams?

In comparison to your talented child, do you make any sacrifices for your other children?

Children who progress rapidly, are constant winners, and provide consistent positive feedback to their parents naturally garner more positive attention. Knowing this, it takes a concerted effort to let the other children in the family know that they too are special and loved.

Culture and Sacrifice

Culture and ethnic background play an important role in terms of what is considered acceptable sacrifice by all parts of the family system: the parents, the highly talented child, and the siblings. For example, traditional Chinese or Indian families may devalue the importance of females and favor a talented male over the equally talented female. Similarly, the level of expected sacrifice for the common good of the family may be very high. The major motivator being the shame, should the sacrifice not be forthcoming. As cultural and ethnic groups assimilate into a country such as the United States, some of these values that are not congruent with the general society may slowly change.

ADVICE FROM THE EXPERTS

It is not easy to weigh the cost of the childhood, parental, and sibling sacrifices necessary to raise a high-achieving child. We talked to a few experts in the field about their opinions on this issue. The experts are (1) John Hodges, director of marketing and public relations for the Amateur Athletic Union (AAU), (2) Robert Sternberg, Ph.D., professor of psychology and education at Yale University, and (3) Peter Libman, director of student life at the School of American Ballet in New York City.

Athletics

We asked John Hodges, director of marketing and public relations for the Amateur Athletic Union (AAU), to tell us his views on the sacrifices young athletes and their families make today to excel in athletics.

"Families of young athletes often make big sacrifices when it comes to time and money. It's of phenomenal interest right now that marketers like apparel and shoe companies, beverage companies, and other corporate sponsors are changing their marketing strategies from focusing on endorsements from high-profile, professional athletes to the 'soccer moms' out there. These are the parents of kids in any sport who are willing to dedicate all their free time to running their kids around and spending big money on sports equipment and clothing. In this good economy, parents have shown that they are willing to pay top price for the best golf clubs, or tennis sneakers, or even a gym bag to give their kids a professional image.

"There are also many parents who make large financial investments in their kids that are somewhat of a gamble. I think the willingness of parents to spend thousands of dollars on their children's sport careers has a lot to do with the financial gains that come with success in the sports world. I can see that parents are more willing to spend $10,000 on their basketball players than they are on soccer players because the payout for the top basketball players in terms of college scholarships, pro contracts, and endorsements is so much higher. The dollars that are laid out in front of top athletes is the driving force behind the sacrifices that thousands and thousands of families make each day. If that money were not out there as an incentive for athletic kids, it's possible that they would be having a much happier childhood doing lots of other things and enjoying more free time. But when you give Tiger Woods a five-year, $25 million contract to sell Buicks, you entice young athletes and their parents to go for this kind of gold.

"Deciding whether to invest a lot of money in a child's athletic experience is a lot like playing the lottery. How much and how often you're willing to pay out depends on how much you hope to get back. If the lottery payout is $5 million, the ticket sales might be one thousand an hour; if the payout is $70 million, they jump to forty-five thousand a minute. The greater the pot, the bigger the risk people are willing to take. When the jackpot in the Florida lottery was $70 million, I saw people who I know have a hard time making their daily expenses laying down $50 and $100 bills to buy a chance at making big money. That turned out to be a bad gamble, because only three people won. Well, in the same way, only seven or eight young girls are going to the Olympics with the gymnastics team, so for an awful lot of families it can be a risky gamble to invest too much money in that dream.

"If you're going to make sacrifices for your child, you have to have a realistic view of why you're doing it. If you can't afford to invest, it'll drive you crazy and may cause adverse actions toward your children. You may demand more, expect more, and drive the children harder in order to make sure they excel and reach the goals you feel are needed in order to reach *your* expected or desired payout. You have to be able to afford to take the risk. If you make all decisions based on the need to get your child to the top, more than likely it will backfire on you. You have to take the approach that 'my child is having fun, I'm having fun, we're meeting a lot of people, we're enjoying this, and even if it doesn't go any further than this, it's been worth it.' When that happens, that kid will have a great time and have a better chance of really making it. Putting pressure on kids like, 'I'm spending this money on you; you've got to make it work,' will destroy the whole concept.

"It's not only the parents who are making sacrifices. The kids too are willing to sacrifice their free time to practice and play their sport. Kids today also have to sacrifice some of the fun of playing lots of different sports. I'm sorry to say that for 90 percent of young athletes, the day of the well-rounded, three-sport athlete is gone. In today's youth sports world, kids can play their sport year round, and that puts demands on their time that won't allow for other 'distractions.' Kids today can compete in sports like baseball, basketball, soccer, and track all year round. There are also skill clinics and strength-training programs geared to each particular sport, which athletes are expected to participate in if they want to excel. The fact is that if you're going to be a good soccer player, for example, you've got to work at it more than just three months out of the year. It's a reasonable sacrifice these days for an exceptional athlete to be a one-sport player.

"The easiest way to judge the value of a sacrifice is, of course, in retrospect. I remember years ago being at an awards banquet, sitting at the table with Tiger Woods's father. A reporter asked him, 'How much do you spend per year on Tiger's pursuit of a golfing career?' Mr. Woods responded that he would figure somewhere in the $50,000 per year range. The reporter said he thought that was pretty foolish, which prompted Mr. Woods to tell him to 'check with me in a few years and see how foolish I am.' Of course with the American Express, Nike, Titleist, and most recently the Buick deal, all worth about $75 to $100 million, I guess Mr. Woods knew what he was working toward. The sad thing about this kind of story is what I've said about the lottery: not all people benefit the same from a gamble, and therefore it

From the Parents' Point of View

"I received a quote from the president of one of our associations (I don't now recall who it was exactly) which said something very memorable. The quote read, 'For young amateur athletes, the joy is in the participation; the agony of defeat is in the mind of the parent.'"

John Hodges, director of marketing and public relations for the AAU

is very important that the youth's happiness be considered above all of this rainbow chasing."

Academics

Robert Sternberg, Ph.D., is a professor of psychology and education at Yale University. He is also the associate director of the National Research Center on Gifted and Talented Education. We asked him to share his feelings about the many opportunities in after-school and summer programs offered to academically bright children.

"There are no hard-and-fast rules about the value of taking extracurricular classes. The good that comes out of summer and after-school programs depends on the quality of the program. Some are very good for kids, and others are no more than test-cramming machines. The question is not, Is it worth enrolling in a Saturday or summer academic program? but rather, What's the quality of the program? Parents don't have to jump on every opportunity that comes by. They need to be more discerning when they enroll their children in academic programs that take up a child's free time.

"Parents also have to answer the question, Am I maintaining balance in my child's life? It's my opinion that it's not in a child's best interest to do too much of any one thing. After a while there are diminishing returns. Parents need to help their children find a balance that will set the precedent for what kind of person they will be as adults. This is hard to do for parents who get too hyper about college acceptance. But academic records, classes, and camps aren't the only route to a higher education. Kids are also accepted because of their interest in music, or art, or gardening, or photography, or carpentry, or whatever. Parents should let their kids do as many activities as possible to find out what they like to do. Just because a child thinks he wants to major in computer science doesn't mean he shouldn't be exploring many other things as well. Parents should encourage their children to find the path that's best for them—not the one that's of most interest to the parents. Kids eventually have to find their own way into a place that's a good fit for them. Part of the challenge of being a good parent is letting them do that."

Performing Arts

The School of American Ballet in New York City is an elite dance school, training students ages eight to twenty. The dancers accepted into this program are exceptionally talented, disciplined, and independent. We asked Peter Libman, director of student life, to tell us about the sacrifices these young people make to become professional dancers.

"There's no denying that exceptionally talented dancers grow up very fast. I don't want to say that they're sacrificing their childhood, but even before they get here, these kids have given all their free time after school and on weekends to the ballet studio, sometimes until nine at night, and have given up typical kid things like hanging out with friends and going to school activities. Then when they get accepted here on the advanced level, they have to make adult, career decisions (often between the ages of about fourteen and sixteen) that their peers may not make until after they're out of college.

"When dancers get to our advanced level and agree that they want to dance full time, their academic hours must revolve around their dance training. They have to make a decision that dance training will come first in their life, because a typical day for an advanced student is pretty demanding. For example, they might get up and have breakfast at 7:30 in the morning; then walk a few blocks over to their academic school to take classes from 8:05 until 10:00; then walk back to our school for a dance class from 10:30 to noon; then grab lunch on the go and return to their academic school from 12:30 to 2:00; then come back to our school for a dance class from 2:30 to 4:00 with possibly a rehearsal from 4:00 to 6:00. They have dinner and then often another practice in the evening, and then it's homework time and to bed. (The dance classes run six days a week.) These kids are very dedicated, and there just isn't a lot of time to do other things. These are not kids who are playing three varsity sports and doing other things most kids do. That's the sacrifice they're making to become professional dancers.

"That doesn't mean we want them to lose sight of other options. We work hard with the kids and their families to emphasize the need to recognize that there is more to life than just dance.

In the past, it wasn't uncommon for young dancers to quit school at sixteen or to earn a diploma through a GED program or correspondence school, but now we really want each of our students to get a good education and to have the opportunity to socialize with other students and teachers who have passions outside the dance world. They shouldn't be sheltered or isolated. And because there are so many variables that make a career in dance uncertain, they should have a good education behind them. We also want them to have other interests and hobbies, even though their time is limited. We ask former dancers to come in and talk to our students about life after dance. When they meet a dancer who is now a lawyer or a photographer, they realize that being a dance teacher when a performance career is over is not the only option. They have to keep their mind open to lots of life's possibilities.

"Most of the students I work with are exceptional in many ways that transfer easily to pursuits outside of dance. They have so much going for them in terms of discipline, persistence, intellect, and drive that I have no doubt that they can be successful in any area they choose."

Look Beyond the Talent into the Future

All parents wonder what the future holds for their children. Will they be happy? Successful? Wealthy? Productive? These are all natural questions that only time will answer. The parents of exceptionally talented and high achieving children ask themselves these same questions—with added wrinkles. They wonder if all the commitment and all the time spent on talent development will bring their children happiness. They wonder if their children will continue to enjoy their special talent years from now. They wonder if their children will be able to have a successful career in their specialized area. They wonder if their exceptional young athletes, scholars, and performing artists are good enough to rise above the crowd and stand out as an adult in the same way they have done throughout their childhood. They wonder if their child can develop a strong and fulfilling social life that parallels their career success.

We are all encouraged by the many stories of young achievers who go on to live exceptional lives. We hear of young Richard Feynman, the Nobel Prize–winning physicist, whose father "knew" his infant boy would be a scientist of great renown. We enjoy the childhood tales of resilient fighters like Wilma Rudolph, who could not walk normally until the age of eleven due to childhood pneumonia, polio, and scarlet fever, but went on to be a track star who won three Olympic gold medals. We admire celebrities like Michael Jackson and Ron Howard for their lifetime achievement of entertaining us from their childhood on. And we hold in awe the careers but not necessarily the lives of prodigies like Mozart and Bobby Fischer.

But we shouldn't ignore the lesser-known stories of those early bloomers who got lost in the shuffle between childhood and adulthood—those whose life story is told in the line, "What ever happened to so-and-so?" Remember Brien Taylor? Probably not, but in 1991 he was big news. At that time, Taylor was a high school senior and the Yankees' number one draft pick; his million-dollar deal was front-page news. From there his athletic career stumbled and fell flat; he never made it out of the minors. What about Dana Plato? She was the young star of the hit TV show *Diff'rent Strokes* who fell into oblivion when the show ended and was not heard from again until she hit the porn circuit; she fell into drugs and alcohol and finally ended her life with a drug overdose in 1999. Sadly, her story is not at all unique. A recent edition of *Politically Incorrect* (ABC, 1999) gathered together childhood stars such as Danny Bonaduce of *The Partridge Family* (who has had several run-ins with the law over drug use) and Gary Coleman of *Diff'rent Strokes* (who was recently charged with assault and filed for bankruptcy) so that they could air their feelings about being conditioned in childhood to need attention and approval as a sign of worth and about the pain of losing that attention as adults. No one told them that the vast majority of indi-

Rick Schroder's Secret

When asked by a reporter how he successfully made the transition from child superstar of the TV show *Silver Spoons* to adult star of TV's *NYPD Blue*, Rick Schroder had a ready answer: "I've been very blessed. My parents always told me I could be anything I wanted. When you grow up in a household like that, you learn to believe in yourself. Consequently, my ego and self-esteem have never been locked up just in acting. So, when I'm succeeding or failing, I'm the same person. This is merely what I do. It's not who I am" (Seligson, 2000, p. 5).

Early Ripe, Early Rot Theory

We don't believe in the "early ripe, early rot" theory that says that hothouse children who bloom very early will lose steam and peter out as they get older. But we do believe that children who show exceptional potential early in life need special help handling the sometimes debilitating pressures of growing up in a fishbowl. They need to be given the opportunity and the tools to develop their chosen area of talent as well as the flexibility and the adaptive skill to turn to other activities. They also need to be given the freedom to be children. They need adults in their lives who will encourage without pushing and who will give love with no strings attached.

viduals who enjoy the spotlight in childhood spend very unassuming adult lives. They admit they did not know how to make that transition. Is your child going to be able to make the adjustment from wonder child to mature adult without major emotional conflict?

The transition from exceptional child to successful adult is complex and difficult for many. It can be a perilous journey that is accompanied by extreme emotional and physical adjustment. Some make it through unscathed; others don't. So one must ask the question, Is there anything parents can do to help their high-achieving children become fulfilled, healthy, and sane adults? The answer is yes. Although it is true that only time will truly tell what the future holds, the following strategies are ones that I have found helpful in guiding children successfully through the often treacherous transition.

Nurture the Whole Child

To guide our children into adulthood successfully, we must be able to look beyond the talent and see the whole child. The goal is for your children to cross the threshold into adulthood physically and mentally secure. If that person happens also to be very talented and able to make a career in her highly specialized area, that's a wonderful bonus.

This philosophy of nurturing whole beings rather than mere technicians is catching on in some surprising places. In the nation's most rigorous academic, music, and dance schools, there is a growing sensitivity to the harm that can be done to the quality of a person's future life when emphasis is placed exclusively on the development of a singular talent.

Consider, for example, the recent change in philosophy at the renowned Juilliard School, one of America's premiere performing arts postsecondary schools, located in New York City. At one time the Juilliard School was a model of the competitive hothouse environment where students learned technical virtuosity and cared about little else. In her book *Nothing but the Best: The Struggle for Perfection at the Juilliard School* (1987), Judith Kogan proclaimed, "Juilliard does not care whether they can tie their shoes, crack an egg or boil a pot of water. Juilliard does not care whether they can screw in a light bulb, mend a fence, or feed a cat. Juilliard does not seem to care whether they can put an English sentence together either. Juilliard cares about whether they can do one thing: perform" (p. 11). Those were the old days at Juilliard. According to Joseph Polisi, the most recent president of Juilliard, things are different now. A hallmark of his tenure has been an evident concern for the physical, psychological, and social well-being of the students. With the goal of producing well-rounded individuals and artists, the school now counsels students to practice hard but also to make sure that their mental and spiritual development keeps pace with the physical and technical (Oestreich, 1999).

Children are not automatons who exist solely to become proficient vehicles showcasing a particular activity or skill. They must never feel this way. As the demanding institutions of perfection take a step back and recognize that all human beings have emotional, social, physical, and psychological needs, we as parents too must look beyond our child's talent and keep in mind the other, less tangible, things that human beings need in order to have fulfilling lives. Our children will be better equipped to deal with the present and the future if we make sure that they know we will love them whether or not they become rich and famous or powerful and successful. All children have the right to be loved for who they are, not what they do. If we can accomplish this, they will be more likely to enter into adulthood with a sound body and mind.

From Prodigy to Adult

"The transition from child musical prodigy to the adult world frequently entails a temporary withdrawal from the artistic pursuit and may suddenly end in emotional defeat and mental anguish or in some extreme cases the complete abandonment of music" (Fisher, 1973).

Be Realistic

Children who excel in athletics, academics, or the performing arts have such wonderful dreams. They see the professionals on TV, in magazines, in movies, and on stage. They close their eyes and imagine themselves in the spotlight. It is this dream that pushes many of them to work so hard, to practice so long, and to persist when those of lesser ambition would give up. These dreams fuel their motivation to be the best.

Children need to dream, and if they want to shoot for the stars, no one should stop them. But as their parents, we need to temper our own idealized view of those dreams with a good dose of reality. Adults need to acknowledge the fact that there is limited room at the very top. This fact is especially apparent in the world of athletics:

There are nearly 1 million high school football players and about 500,000 basketball players. Of that number, each year about 150 eventually make it through college to the NFL, and about 50 make an NBA team.

For boys, there are 270 Division I colleges offering baseball scholarships. Each school is allowed to award 3 freshmen a scholarship. With 107,000 high school seniors playing the sport, the odds of receiving a scholarship are 1 in 132.

For girls, there are 90 Division I colleges offering soccer scholarships. Each school is allowed to award 3 to 4 freshmen scholarships. With 37,500 high school seniors playing the sport, the odds of receiving a scholarship are 1 in 119.

The odds of a high school football player making it to the pros at all—let alone having a career—are about 6,000 to 1; the odds for a high school basketball player are 10,000 to 1.

Even for those talented and fortunate enough to play at the professional level, careers are typically short lived. The average active tenure in the NFL is 3.2 years, yet a player must be in the NFL for 4.5 years to qualify for a pension and be fifty-five years old to draw on it!

In the United States, 2 million children and adolescents participate in competitive gymnastics per year, and just 7 or 8 participate in the Olympic games every four years.

These statistics illustrate why we have an obligation to attempt to ensure that even children with superior talent have a well-rounded developmental experience. No matter how good they are in one particular area, they must be fully prepared for life. Children need to know that the world won't end if they don't reach their first goal. They need to feel in their bones that they are a valuable person who can use their talent and skills to find life satisfaction in many ways. Many musicians who don't make it to the concert stage build fine careers for themselves as members of the city orchestra, as composers, as music producers, and as studio musicians, and many spend their whole lives enjoying and playing music on a personal, amateur, or local level. Thousands of athletes who don't make it to professional ranks or who do so for a very short period find fulfilling related careers in broadcasting, sports reporting, sports agenting, sports photography, sports law, and on and on. Others continue to be physically active and enjoy athletics on a

Have a Plan B

"The music performance majors I teach at the College of Arts at California State University all think at first that they're going to play first chair in the New York Philharmonic. But they rapidly begin to realize that in every college in the country there is another musician who will be trying out for that same seat who is just as good as they are. Performers need to have an alternative plan."

Deborah Mitchell, D.M.A., director of music education at the College of the Arts at California State University, Long Beach

fun, healthy level for the rest of their lives. Thousands upon thousands of young scholars who don't get admitted into their first choice of universities or who don't get the job offers they expected find happiness and success in other places.

In my practice, I often work with families and children who have lost sight of the world that exists beyond their narrow area of talent. I have found that they need to understand that the skills and knowledge developed in pursuit of their goal can serve them well in a variety of other disciplines or vocations. The experience of regular, hard-driven effort makes an individual a more disciplined and hard-working person forever. The experience of standing before an audience to compete, perform, or debate paves the way to make every other kind of presentation or public appearance in adulthood easier to handle. None of this training is "wasted" if the child falls short of the top.

Adults and coaching mentors who are caught in Achievement by Proxy Distortion (ABPD) traps are blinded to a greater reality. They can't even think about the possibility of their own lives without the glory (or the financial gains) of the spotlight. But parents who do not depend on their children's success for their own sense of self and achievement are able both to encourage a child to reach high for a dream and to build a realistic Plan B safety net.

Beware the Downside of Competition

High-achieving children live in a highly competitive world. Some people feel that this kind of life has a positive influence on a person's skill development and is an important part of learning early on to hang tough under the pressure of the adult world. Others fear that competition in youth activities can cause developmental burnout and fear of competitive situations in adult life. The reality is that competition in and of itself is not what affects the future development of your child, either for good or ill. The danger or value of competition depends on how adults and their young charges use, value, process, and digest competition during the growing years.

Especially when children are young, competition must be enjoyable, challenging, and fun. Very young children are not very competitive by nature. Imposing rules, regulations, scoreboards, standings, and championships into their "play" ruins the joy. Better, early on, that children learn about rules by developing their own. Parents and children lose sight of their goal to develop a skill and instead get caught up in the race to be the best and to win a league or state title, national championship, scholarship, blue ribbon, or headline. Unfortunately, when the pleasure and fun of the process is gone, so often goes the desire to do well, the willingness to work at talent development, and the ability to stay on top.

The world loses many talented people to the competitive burnout that occurs in childhood. If you would like to see your child continue to grow in her area of special talent and enjoy its benefits when she hits the teen years and beyond, be careful of the kind and number of competitions she is exposed to at an early age. In some circumstances competition can destroy self-esteem and desire, but in others it can be a skill builder and a motivator. The outcome depends on your ability to foster and model a *mastery-oriented* attitude toward competition rather than an *ego-oriented* one.

Ego Orientation

The effect that early competition will have on the long-term adjustment of a person often depends on the type of competitive personality he has. Through the example of instructors and parents, children learn to be either ego oriented or mastery oriented.

The ego- or outcome-oriented person ties her self-esteem and identity into winning. Losing is to be avoided at all costs because it is embarrassing, demeaning, and shameful. Beating others in a competitive setting is how the ego-oriented person gains a sense of competence. In fact, the ego-oriented person will drop out of an activity as soon as she begins to lose, or sometimes before she has a chance to lose. This person would rather not participate at all than bear the pain that losing causes when it dashes the personal perception of self-esteem and self-worth tied to a single activity.

Because winning is the strongest motivation behind ego-oriented individuals, they are often open to the pressure to cheat or take shortcuts in order to succeed. These individuals may take performance-enhancing drugs, steal test answers, and lie and cheat if that's what it takes to win. This brings to mind headline-grabbing stories such as that of top-ranked skater Tanya Harding, who was banned from the U.S. Figure Skating Association for participating in a conspiracy to intentionally damage the knees of her rival, Nancy Kerrigan, a few weeks before the 1994 Winter Olympics. An ego-oriented person can be driven to even criminal lengths to come out on top.

Usually children learn from influential adults how to be an ego-oriented competitor. Mike, for example, was raised to be a winner. "I remember running to my father when I was little to show him the second-place ribbon I had won in a track meet. He put it down on the table saying, 'When it's a first-place ribbon, then I'll get excited.' That comment pushed me to work harder until I did win first place—over and over again for years. I was the best on every track team I ever joined. But that one comment also taught me that winning was all that mattered. Not how hard I worked, not how well I performed, not how much I learned and improved. I still have trouble with any kind of competition. I'm so afraid I might not be the best that I turn down many opportunities in my adult life that could benefit my career and my personal life, but I'm just too afraid of losing, so I don't even try."

Is It "Part of the Game"?

During a youth hockey game in Chicago in November 1999, fifteen-year-old Neal Goss was smacked in the back with a hockey stick by a rival player, causing him to careen into the boards that surround the rink, severing his spinal cord. Goss was left paralyzed; the other boy was charged with aggravated battery and now faces five years in juvenile detention. The boy's lawyers insist that he rammed his rival as "part of a game." Goss's lawyers insist, "The kid wasn't merely attempting to play hockey but intending to hurt his opponent" (Cohen, 2000, p. 26). It looks as though the legal courts are starting to take a hard look at this kind of game violence. In February 2000, eighteen-year-old Tony Limon was sentenced to five years in prison for throwing a vicious elbow to the face of an opponent during a high school basketball game in San Antonio, Texas. These cases spotlight the issue of whether or not how you play the game is as important as winning the game and whether hostile aggression is an acceptable part of youth sports.

As Mike has learned, being an ego-oriented competitor severely constricts creative learning opportunities. With winning as the end goal, there is no room for creativity, risk taking, or experimentation. Those who are so afraid of making a mistake can only struggle to reach their full potential.

Mastery Orientation

The mastery- or process-oriented person, in contrast, wants to be as good as he can possibly be, regardless of whether he wins or loses. (This is also referred to as being process oriented.) Personal improvement is the primary goal, and competition pushes this person to work harder and perform better to meet his own internal set of standards. These individuals usually are willing to put more time into practice and rehearsal and study than are ego-oriented individuals, who are focused only on the final outcome. Mastery-oriented competitors can lose the competition and still feel good about their performance. They can enjoy the gains they've made and the knowledge they've gathered, even if someone else takes home first place. Mastery-oriented competitors have respect for their opponents and themselves, even if they lose. They are motivated by a desire to become excellent in a chosen area. They are open to learning new skills and trying new methods and approaches, and they do not worry obsessively that a loss will knock them out of the running.

Henry is a mastery-oriented pianist. At the age of ten he entered his first competition, and although he didn't even place, he loved it. It gave him an opportunity to compare himself to other young pianists and set a goal toward which to work. He begged his teacher to sign him up for another one and immediately redoubled his practice efforts. He also enjoyed going to hear pianists in concert, where he could learn by watching different techniques and hearing different kinds of music. It wasn't long before Henry began making a name for himself in the music world. His teacher and parents were happy to see how fiercely competitive he was, yet they were always surprised that he never took a mistake or a lost competition as a sign of failure. These setbacks always gave him a reason to practice harder. Henry wanted to be an excellent pianist. He didn't need to be a renowned one or a famous one; those things could come as a natural consequence of working so hard to achieve a personal goal.

These two approaches have been well studied by researchers for many years. There is ample evidence that the mastery-oriented individual is best equipped to handle the pressures of competition both in the world of the high-achieving child and then later in the highly competitive and sometimes cutthroat adult world.

In 1993, Rena Subotnik and colleagues designed a study to assess the long-term outcomes of early identification and schooling for a group of highly gifted children (Subotnik, 1997). Their focus group consisted of people now in their forties and fifties who had been selected at the age of four to attend one of America's most selective educational institutions, the Hunter College Elementary School in New York, which was created in 1941 to serve children with exceptionally high IQ scores. Those surveyed were asked to describe the competitive environment of their elementary school. Most found the pressure of competition to be a negative factor in their schooling, as these excerpts show (Subotnik, 1997):

> I think that the stiff competition and the constant striving to be better turned what could have been a very positive experience into something with very, very negative side effects. I wish children could take the good out of it, which there was a lot of, but remove the competitive environment. . . . I think that the competitiveness and the environment that was set up there was a real hindrance to me later, in that, for example, now I won't even play a game of tennis.

An Added Burden

"Can winning or losing a competition be too much to bear for the maturing prodigy? Doesn't adolescence have sufficient confusion, loss of esteem, and manic, grandiose, despairing energy of its own without this added burden? Despite the promise of success, fame, and financial gain, in many cases what the young musician needs is shelter and safety" (Kenneson, 1998, p. 189).

I just like to hit the ball. I'm really kind of burned out, I think because of all the competition I felt in grade school [forty-three-year-old female, p. 60].

One of the largest negative aspects, I think, is the level of competition that was introduced at all levels of the curriculum. We were being told that we individually had to do well, which meant in effect that we were being compared constantly to each other as individuals. I think we failed to learn to work as a group, failed to really see group projects or group efforts rewarded, and in my later life I certainly felt that to be a strong disadvantage in the way the real world operates [thirty-eight-year-old female, p. 61].

Watch Those Social Skills

The child who is very comfortable performing superbly on the stage, in the classroom, or on the playing field may not feel quite as relaxed doing "simple" social activities taken for granted by peers who are leading a more normal and less rarefied life.

Making long-term friends, for example, can be very difficult for the high-achieving child. If his talent puts him on a level "too high" above other kids his age, classmates may have no common interests or may shun him because he is "different"—and often he is. Children who spend hours each day developing their talent neglect the learning and practice of age-appropriate socialization skills. Like any child who has been brought up in an isolated or elite environ-

Beyond Mensa and Test Grades

"The research tells us that there is much more to the making of a gifted person than the abilities revealed on traditional tests of intelligence, aptitude, and achievement. Furthermore, history tells us it has been the creative and productive people of the world, the producers rather than consumers of knowledge, the reconstructionists of thought in all areas of human endeavor, who have become recognized as 'truly gifted' individuals. History does not remember persons who merely scored well on IQ tests or those who learned their lessons well" (Renzulli, 1998).

ment, they don't know how to take turns, share, and listen empathically to others. They spend inordinate amounts of time in the company of grownups and often dress and speak in an adult manner. These children may not have the time or the interest to relate to the latest kid craze or fad. They often crave adult approval and are ridiculed by peers for "kissing up" to teachers and instructors. High-achieving children may also be scorned and isolated simply because they are exceptionally talented "nerds," making some insecure children and their parents feel threatened and jealous.

Exceptional children are sometimes set apart from their peers because they may not live by the same set of rules that govern everyone else's growing-up years. When everybody else has to get homework done, the talented dancer or musician may be excused because she needs the time to rehearse. When everybody else is doing family chores, the proficient scholar may be allowed to study for the big test. When everybody else is sweating out how to get a date for the school dance, the talented athlete is getting to sleep early in preparation for the competition the next day. This "exempt" and entitled status sets these individuals up for a fall when they cross over into adulthood. Suddenly they are not so special, and they are expected to fill out the same forms and do the same work as everyone else on the job. Suddenly no one is doing the chores for them, and their household is a mess. Suddenly they have to figure out how to initiate and maintain human relationships. Developing the social and life skills that are required of adults takes effort and know-how that is rooted in childhood.

Because of this exceptional treatment, it is very easy for precocious children to become self-centered and selfishly egotistical. For example, twelve-year-old Catherine is a top figure skater and shows promise of being one of the few who might make it to the Olympics. She is very proud of herself, with good reason, but the pride has turned to self-adulation. She knows that in her family the sun rises and sets on her accomplishments. She is loved for what she does, and she does it well. Her mother laughs with pride when Catherine shows signs of conceit by saying things like, "I'm not worried about this little competition; there's no one around here better than me." She smiles indulgently and approvingly when she sees Catherine primping for hours in front of the mirror in her new skating outfits and theatrical makeup. Her dad has elevated her to the status of superstar by refusing to ask her to do some chores around the house. "My little skater can't risk hurting herself by tripping over a broom," he laughs. When Catherine talks to her parents rudely or refuses to follow their wishes, they let her have her way, fearing that making her upset will throw off her concentration when she skates. Focusing on Catherine the figure skater rather than Catherine the growing child, these well-meaning parents have created their own social monster. Very few in her teen life or beyond into her adult life will put up with her self-centered attitude. Catherine will eventually find out that an egotistical star is unwelcome in any social circumstance outside the family that nurtured it. Exceptional children do need to be confident and self-assured to survive in their competitive world, but they don't need to be spoiled and bratty. There are very few John McEnroes who can get away with such behavior.

If this situation becomes the norm, this child will likely have trouble adjusting to the adult world, where it's no longer "cute" to be socially inept. In fact, the adjustment can be quite painful. Inadequate social skills are more noticeable and debilitating in the late teenage years or twenties as children try to bridge the gap to adulthood. Sometimes the problem persists throughout the person's lifetime.

As you watch your child grow in his area of specialized talent, also monitor how his all-round social skills develop. Remember that he is always a person before he is any kind of circus freak; he is a person who has to live realistically in the world with other people. Teach him good manners, responsibility, and respect for others. Encourage interests outside his area of talent so he can have social conversations and shared activities with peers. Allow downtime for

Peer Problems

"The problems of adolescence are compounded by the prodigy's belonging half to the adult world and half to the world of the children about him. While the prodigy mathematician Norbert Wiener had suspected that adults viewed him as an oddity, he suffered terribly as an adolescent when he realized that his peers held much the same view" (Fisher, 1973, p. 45).

play and fun and social interaction. Your child deserves to learn how to enjoy the company, friendship, and support of his peers.

Minimize Chronic Stress

Stress is part of everyday existence, even for children. There's stress in deciding what to wear and with whom to make friends. There's stress in taking school tests and trying out for sport teams. There's stress in performing in the school choir or at a dance recital. Meeting these stressful situations and coming out whole teaches children the value of taking risks to gain pride and a feeling of accomplishment. But stress also has an ugly and destructive side when it is unrelenting. Chronic stress is at the top of the list of things that diminish the likelihood of long-term future success in a given area.

The pressure of consistently being a high achiever can destroy a child's dreams in several ways:

- Stress can reduce the enjoyment of the activity. It is well studied and understood that children need fun and play in any challenging activity in order to persist at it willingly. Unfortunately, both the value and meaning of play are poorly understood in our hurried society. Indeed, this generation has transformed play into work. What was once recreational—sports, summer camp, musical training—is now professionalized, competitive, and consequently very stressful.

- Stress can hurt children's performance. When children's anxiety level is very high, it is difficult for some to learn and retain information and skills, making it difficult for them to perform well. Ironically, these children's exceptional abilities put them in such high stress situations that their performance suffers, and they begin to look quite average.

- Stress can lead to increased risk of illness and injury. A highly anxious or nervous person expends much physical and mental energy on the distraction created by stress. The negative effects of stress on the immune system are well known. Chronic stress opens the individual to many illnesses and disorders (such as colds, flu, fatigue, depression, headaches, and stomachaches) that interfere with the development of potential. Athletes and performing artists are more easily and more often injured when they are nervous and unable to concentrate calmly on the performance of the skill.

- Stress increases the likelihood of dropout. Children who are chronically stressed are less willing to put in the time and effort required to develop their talent. They drop out because of a combination of all the reasons we've already listed: they're not having fun; they're no longer performing up to their potential or to the expectations of their parents or instructors; their illnesses or injuries cause them to fall behind in their lessons or training, and they get too discouraged to make the extra effort needed to catch up.

- High-achieving children and young adults are expected to—and learn very well how to—take significant risks physically and emotionally for their chosen activity, not unlike traumatized children. Not surprising, this risk taking, which may benefit them in the one arena, extends to other parts of their lives. Under the chronic stress of their often ungrounded precocious careers, normal adolescent risk taking can be exaggerated. Like Icarus, these high flyers willingly risk everything. Jennifer Capriati's shoplifting and drug convictions, Oxana Baiul's drunk driving arrest, and the death of NBA star Bobby Phills caused by drag racing his luxury car spring to mind.

Perhaps the most serious problem is that patterns of coping with stress established in childhood can be carried over into adulthood and become chronic. The child who gets tension headaches can, in all likelihood, become the adult who experiences migraine

Risky Behaviors

In the area of risk, safety, and lifestyle, researchers (Stryer, Tofler, and Lapchick, 1998) have compared college athletes with age-matched peers. The behaviors they compared included alcohol use; driving under the influence of drugs and alcohol; getting into a car with an impaired driver; use of seat belts; use of helmets on bikes, mopeds, or motorcycles; use of contraception; number of sexual partners; and sexually transmitted diseases. The athletes were shown to exhibit a significantly higher proportion of risky lifestyle behaviors.

headaches or panic attacks. The child with stomach pains may become the adult with chronic anxiety-related colitis. Excessive stress in childhood can have lifelong effects by producing a debilitating pattern of anxiety-related physical illness.

Children who are objectified by adults caught in ABPD traps may be left to deal with the stress of high-level performance on their own. This situation sets the stage for the development of maladaptive coping styles that make it that much more difficult for children to fulfill their potential.

Janine, for example, gradually lost her "honors student" status when her complaints about headaches were ignored. Early in the third grade, Janine began to complain of headaches whenever she was scheduled to take a test at school. Because Janine always earned exceptional grades on all her tests, her stiff-upper-lip parents were surprised by her whining. "What are you worried about?" they'd ask her. "You always get very good grades. Now get off to school and take that test." The stress-related migraines on those days were unbearable for Janine, and her grades began to drop. The more her parents scolded her for having headaches "for no good reason" and then for getting poor grades, the more the headaches interfered with her schoolwork. In response to this tense situation, her body and mind generated an automatic psychosomatic response of an unbearable headache, creating a vicious cycle that would follow Janine into her teen and early adult years.

We can help our young high achievers avoid excessive and chronic stress symptoms by recognizing the problem as soon as possible and breaking the response pattern before it becomes automatic and difficult to change. This intervention begins with two relatively simple steps:

1. *Talk about the stress symptoms and the high expectations that may be causing them.* Children cannot be perfect all the time. If they expect to be (or if we expect them to be), naturally they will be under constant stress. Ask your young scholar to visualize what will happen if he gets a B on a test. Ask your athlete to imagine making a play that loses the game. Encourage your performing artist to mentally walk through her performance and imagine what she will do if she makes a mistake. Help your child understand that life will go on and that you will still love her. Encourage her to see that mistakes are natural

and wonderful learning opportunities. Tell her stories about famous people (for example, Albert Einstein, Michael Jordan, and the Wright Brothers) who initially missed the mark but with persistence eventually achieved their goal. Show her the excellent documentary *Hoop Dreams,* which shows real, highly talented adolescents and their families coping with adversity, dealing with failures, and readjusting their goals in the face of changing realities. Kids need to know that there is also no shame in giving it their best shot and sometimes coming up short. They need to know that we do not expect them to do everything perfectly all the time and that they should not expect that of themselves. Knowing this takes a world of pressure off a child's shoulders.

2. *Teach your child relaxation response exercises.* One of the most positive things you can do for your exceptional child is to teach him to recognize and short-circuit the negative aspects of the stress response. There are many excellent books written on relaxation strategies, and there are also therapists trained in biofeedback and other relaxation techniques that you might explore further. These skills will serve your child well no matter where he goes in life or how he uses his special talents.

Even young children can train their bodies to relax under pressure. There are three simple exercises you can teach your child today:

- *Positive self-talk.* When your child begins to fret and have negative thoughts—"I'm going to mess up," "I can't do this," and so on—teach her to stop the negative thought and then imagine performing the stressful feat with great success. Let her mentally feel the pride of doing a good job. This kind of positive imagining will calm the body and stop it from tensing up in fear and anxiety, which can tighten muscles and blood vessels, causing headaches and stomachaches. (The books and tapes of psychologist Dr. Terry Orlick can be very helpful in this regard.)
- *Deep breathing.* When we get nervous, we can hyperventilate; that is, our breathing becomes rapid, short, and shallow, which disrupts the normal carbon dioxide and oxygen balance (and, if prolonged, the pH balance in the body). It causes such symptoms as lightheadedness, fainting, nausea, physical weakness, and poor judgment. Teach your child to take slow, deep

breaths and to say reassuring words to himself, such as, "This is fun" or "I'm ready" as he exhales.
* *Guided imagery.* Help your child create a magical place in her mind where she is calm and happy. It should be a place that makes her feel relaxed and glad to be alive. It should be a place with no problems, no expectations, and no tension. Maybe your child's place will be alone on a beach, or maybe it will be in the middle of a party with all her friends. Wherever it is, going there mentally will help her calm down. Once this place has been created, remind your child to go to her special place for just a few minutes at least once a day.

Nurture Your Parent-Child Relationship

There is no debate: being caught in an ABPD trap harms the parent-child relationship. When parents put their own needs and dreams ahead of those of their children, they are headed down a road that is eventually bound to fork; the children will take the escape route that heads away from the path their parents have chosen for them.

In their early teens, children naturally become more critical of their parents and of adults in general. This is their way of pulling away and discovering their own autonomous selves. Children who have been pushed, prodded, and intimidated by their parents, however, can become excessively critical, because they begin to realize they have been somehow used and exploited. They begin to see that their parents are excessively involved in their lives for selfish reasons. They catch on to the fact that they are loved primarily for what they accomplish and for the vicarious pride they bring to the family. They also see that their natural need for some independence is met with extreme resistance by parents who can't bear the thought of losing control over their children. This sets up a power struggle that can have lifelong consequences.

The sports news is bursting with stories about the struggles between young athletes and their overly involved parents. Tennis star Mary Pierce has suffered the humiliation of having her dad banned from the circuit and court-ordered to stay away from his daughter because of his obnoxious tantrums on the court. At the age of seventeen, Olympic gymnast Dominique Moceanu had a restraining order placed against her parents while she sued to achieve legal emancipation from them because of their mismanagement of her earnings. And Venus and Serena Williams's dad has made a crucial life plan decision, announcing that he wants both to be retired from tennis by age twenty-two. The unwillingness of some parents to let their older children and even young adults choose the direction of their own lives has destroyed many families.

High-achieving children are often very perceptive. They know ABPD parents have violated the parent-child "contract," so they may feel no need to fulfill their part of the mutual obligation. They often feel no need to be loyal to their parents nor to the values and beliefs their parents espouse. They may flaunt their anger by disobeying their parents, by breaking house rules, by being rude and obnoxious. The arguments escalate as resentment and hostility come to the surface. The child who used to do whatever the parent said, now becomes defiant and may abandon her area of expertise rather than stay caught in the controlling grasp of her parents.

This is the ultimate danger of ABPD. Not only does the child turn away from something that might have given her lifelong enjoyment and a sense of pride and accomplishment, but she also loses the love and support of her parents. She lives with the question her parents throw out in anger: "After all we've done for you, is this how you repay us?" Both parents and child lose something that is priceless and irreplaceable: a loving parent-child relationship.

To successfully make the leap from child star to fulfilled adult, your child needs you to be a parent first and foremost right now— not a coach, not a negotiator, not an agent, not an accountant, not a publicist. A parent. All these other roles should come second, and then only if they can be handled without diluting the primary responsibility to be supportive and nurturing.

ADVICE FROM THE EXPERTS

Competent experts know that it is important to nurture the whole child in order to prepare him or her for a healthy and happy future. We have interviewed three of these experts and share their thoughts with you. They include (1) Lori Hendricks, the coordinator of an education outreach program sponsored by the National Collegiate Athletic Association (NCAA), (2) Joseph S. Renzulli, Ed.D., director of the National Research Center on Gifted and Talented Education, and (3) Lawrence Ferrara, chair of the Department of Music and Performing Arts Professions at New York University.

Athletics

Lori Hendricks is the coordinator of an education outreach program sponsored by the National Collegiate Athletic Association (NCAA), called CHAMPS (Challenging Athlete's Minds for Personal Success)/Life Skills. This program offers services and support to NCAA colleges and universities to encourage the total development of student athletes. We asked her how parents can help their young athletes become fully developed and prepared for life in the future.

"The CHAMPS/Life Skills Program assists with transitional times in a student-athlete's life—particularly the transition from high school to college and then from college to professional careers. There are many social, athletic, and personal demands at these times that cause a lot of stress and may lead one to participate in unhealthy and risky activities. Transitional periods are easier to navigate if a person has developed a sense of community—an understanding that the student-athlete is a member of a much larger group of individuals who need to work together to improve the quality of life. Parents can play a big role in helping their children celebrate a sense of community—within the family unit, within the neighborhood, and within the church. Families should find opportunities for their young athletes to develop healthy relationships and to work outside the home with others for a common cause. Parents can involve their children in community service activities that give them a sense that there is something larger than just 'me.' They can take their children to see different cultural events and give them books to read that support and celebrate multiculturalism. Being a part of an athletic team gives children a sense of group identity, but they need to learn how to connect with a larger community; they need to feel comfortable with and be sensitive toward people who are different from themselves: people who are nonathletes, people with different interests, people from different parts of the country, and people of different races, ethnic origins, and gender. It is very unhealthy to identify yourself only as an athlete and to be isolated from the larger community.

"Talking with children about transitions before they occur is the best thing that parents can do to help young athletes avoid the risky behaviors that so often occur when young people leave home. Families need to have serious dialogues about issues like violence, dangerous drinking, ethics, and sexual responsibility. There are sites on the Web now where parents can obtain lots of information and support to pass along to their children. Parents can also help create workshops in their community to address these issues and then make sure their kids attend. Parents should be involved in their local schools and find out if there is a program for life-skills development. They should identify the resources available to children that will prepare them for life after graduation. There are some very big issues that occur at the college level that need to be addressed at the elementary and high school levels.

"One big issue is the athlete's definition of 'sportsmanship' that he or she will take into adulthood. This is different from the gamesmanship young athletes are learning on the field. Fortunately, involved parents can have some control over the way their young athletes play the game and the way they build a sense of ethics. Parents have to decide if they're willing to support 'game strategies' like ridiculing opponents, trash talking, and breaking the rules. Parents also have to look at the kind of example they give in their daily lives that teaches ethical conduct and sportsmanship. Are values like honesty, respect, and loyalty important to them? Do they sacrifice their integrity to get ahead? Do they lie to their peers? Do they show respect to their colleagues? Do they handle competition with anger and insults? Do they voice their feelings that cheating and verbal abuse are unacceptable? We have to teach our children through example that sportsmanship is important; that's how we give our children an ethical foundation to live with in the world at large.

"A sense of teamwork, discipline, and perseverance, and a healthy sense of the body, are all values that can be taken from youth sports into adulthood. The institution of sports has a great deal of influence in our society today. I think children need their parents to help them use the many positive lessons in sports to build a happy, full, and healthy future for themselves."

Academics

Joseph S. Renzulli, Ed.D., is professor of gifted education and director of the National Research Center on Gifted and Talented Education at the University of Connecticut. We asked Dr. Renzulli to share his experiences with parental expectations for the future of their young scholars.

"When asked, 'What is the one thing you want most for your child?' parents most often will say, 'I want my child to be happy.' But if we probe beyond that, especially in the case of parents who have extremely bright kids, happiness oftentimes is determined by the parents' own goals and expectations. Parents who have children with high potential usually hope that they will go to competitive colleges and enter into challenging careers in one of the more prestigious areas, such as law, medicine, or business. I don't think anyone has done solid research on this, but in my own anecdotal experience, this is what I've seen that parents expect for their kids.

"However, there's always a possibility for conflict over these expectations when the child chooses a different road. The child, for example, who is interested in something that the parents do not consider to be a career that is more in keeping with the traditional society markers for success can find himself or herself in the middle of a major family dispute. 'I'm not going to law school; I want to design clothing,' is the kind of statement that can cause problems for these families. I recall when I graduated from the graduate school at the University of Virginia, a young man who had just gotten his medical degree tossed the diploma to his parents saying, 'There it is. You wanted it; now I'm going into the Peace Corps.' Obviously, there was a wide gap between the parents' expectations and what the young man wanted to do with his life at that time.

"To avoid this kind of conflict, there needs to be a lot of communication between the parent and the young person, especially at important transition points such as when choosing a college and a major. These are key points in time when the parents may have an expectation that the child will pursue medicine, science, engineering, or business, and the child might be more interested in philosophy or humanities or arts. I would not personally force my own children to go in a direction I choose even though I know it would be more financially rewarding, prestigious, and so on, but I know many people who wouldn't bat an eyelash while saying, 'You're going to be a lawyer.'

"It's hard to get past the feeling that parents know what's best and therefore should tell their children what to do. But this belief can cause many difficulties down the road if the child chooses a career based on family pressures rather than personal interests. I believe that people are almost guaranteed a better payoff when they're working in an area that is of very strong personal interest to them. Anyone who has ever become famous has done so because she considers what she does not an occupation but something fun. That's very important. In fact, a better predictor of future success than schoolwork is extracurricular activities. The kinds of things that kids do with their free time are better indicators of what they will accomplish as adults than what they do in the classroom.

"Having said this, the bottom line is that there is no absolutely accurate way to predict future success. There is some controversy in the literature on the relationship between early identification as 'gifted' and adult success. In Terman's *Genetics Studies of Genius,* some gifted individuals fulfilled the promise of their youth, but others did not. We all know people who were valedictorian, most-likely-to-succeed, superstar, and golden boy or girl who ended up parking cars and pumping gas. We also know kids who struggled through school and then dropped out of college and started companies like Microsoft. It's very hard to make predictions for these bright kids. Research, experience, and common sense tell us that kids who do well in elementary school usually do well in high school; kids who do well in high school usually do well in college; kids who do well in college usually go on to satisfying careers. But that doesn't give anyone a guarantee."

Performing Arts

Lawrence Ferrara is a pianist, musicologist, and author, and the chair of the Department of Music and Performing Arts Professions at New York University, which services about eighteen hundred baccalaureate through doctoral students and is one of the largest performing arts programs in the country. We asked Dr. Ferrara to share his insights as someone who for over twenty years has watched performing artists make the leap from student to professional, some very successfully, some not so successfully.

"There's no question that young performing artists are going into a very competitive field and only a small percentage are going to be successful. Our numbers at NYU are an example. Consider the applications for many of our undergraduate programs. This year we will receive over 400 applications from prospective music theater majors and music business majors; we'll accept only 30 in each major. In music technology, we'll receive 180 applications for 18 spots. So just to get into a top performing arts program is extraordinarily competitive. Then how many who graduate will make it in the business professionally? While we have close to a 100 percent job placement record for our music business, technology, and education graduates, it is very different for performance majors. Although many of our graduates are now on Broadway, we know a lot of our kids are not going to be big performing stars. Some will make a good living, but most performing majors usually land in second- or third-tier careers where they often have to supplement their income by doing other nonmusical things.

"This is a painful reality check for individuals who have spent eight to ten hours of every day of their lives at the piano or violin or in the dance studio. That's why I think it's so important for performing artists to get a liberal arts education that prepares them to go beyond their artistic skills. It opens up their eyes and prepares them to understand a rather complex world that sometimes they don't yet fathom.

"It's very difficult in the early stages for many performing arts students to recognize the value of a broad education. They often want to shut out everything else and focus on practicing. They don't care about their other classes or the cultural environment in which they live. Ultimately they find that they are socially and, to an extent, culturally and intellectually crippled because they aren't prepared to deal with the world around them. This is unfortunate because to be successful in the performing arts, 90 percent of young performers have to go to gatherings such as cocktail parties; they have to meet people; they have to be social and gregarious and be equipped to take part in conversations that have nothing to do with their performing art. I think it's particularly important for students to broaden their horizons. This prepares them to be articulate and interesting. It also translates into their performing ability.

"This year I'm teaching an undergraduate class called 'The Performing Arts in Western Civilization,' and my opening remarks to these sixty or so students who major in such areas as theater, composition, jazz, and classical performance emphasize this point. I tell them that if you look at all the successful people in the performing arts, with very few exceptions, you'll find that they are extraordinarily well read; they know a great deal about many different subjects. They are able to bring not only their life experiences but a cultural richness to their performing art. That's the key. It's not only that they will be more holistic people but that their performance will be improved by it as well. You can't be successful in a performance art that ultimately is a reflection of your culture and be isolated from that culture. You need to experience an empathic journey so that your life and your art complement each other. I tell my students that they can't perform in a vacuum; they need to respond to political, social, and religious issues and ideas in life that they can then transform into the language of dance or poetry or music. In order to do that you cannot live your life in the practice room—that's shortsighted and not the formula for success in either the performing arts or life in general."

What is the one thing you want most for your child? Think carefully about your answer to this question. Things like fame, glory, success, and wealth can certainly enrich a person's life, but only if they come after good health and happiness. Your job as a parent is to love and nurture your children so they can achieve health and happiness in their adult life. With these two gifts, they can find their way to all the other things that life has to offer.

Step Six will help you stay alert to the red flags that indicate that your children are suffering from ABPD behaviors that will keep them from becoming productive, healthy, fulfilled, and sane adults.

Step Six

Beware the Red Flags of Achievement by Proxy Distortion

Children who are exceptionally talented in a particular area usually gain much from their abilities and achievements. They develop a sense of self-worth and accomplishment; they have a strengthened sense of identity and derive self-esteem and self-confidence. They feel personal pride and happiness at meeting and exceeding personal goals. They may also bask in the mirror of love and admiration of their parents, peers, and instructors.

If only this idyllic state of positive feedback and motivation could continue throughout childhood for all talented, high-achieving children! The external reinforcement, support, and nurturing that encourage a child to work hard and achieve personal goals often don't last. As we have seen throughout this book, as the ability rises and the stakes increase, underlying adult pressures and demands reveal themselves to an often naive child. The enjoyment or fun factor is at risk of becoming so deeply buried beneath external expectations that the increasingly ambivalent and even cynical child can barely remember why she wanted to develop this talent in the first place. When the stress of constantly meeting other people's needs for reflected glory or even financial support becomes unbearable, children will send out distress signals.

These signals range from mild moodiness to self-destructive behaviors. Supportive parents will recognize and respond to a cry for help; ABPD parents will deny, ignore, or compound the problem.

Burnout

Burnout is an umbrella term for what happens to a child who excels in a certain skill and then loses interest to the point of withdrawing from the activity altogether. The causes of burnout can be all the things we've talked about in this book that turn an enjoyable, rewarding activity into an arduous chore. It can be the training regimen, the demanding attitudes of the parents and instructors, the unrelenting high expectations to perform with injury, the grueling performance schedule, or simply boredom.

A worried mom recently told us the story of her twelve-year-old daughter, Sara, who was a talented pianist. "Although Sara dutifully practiced for two hours every day," she said, "I noticed about a month ago that she wasn't really getting anything out of her practices. She'd play the same things over and over without trying anything new or following her teacher's instructions. Soon she started cutting her practice time short, some days even 'forgetting' to play at all. We began to have awful arguments about her practice habits. And then she made several mistakes when she played at our church last week—something that had never happened before. Shortly after that I saw Sara sitting at the piano, playing a beautiful piece by Mozart with tears rolling down her face. When I asked her what was the matter, she burst out crying and said, 'I'm so sick of playing the piano I can't stand it anymore.' I couldn't believe my ears. Sara is an exceptional musician. How could she not enjoy this gift?"

There may be other things going on in Sara's life that we don't know about, but it sounds like a simple case of burnout. The following are the typical signs of burnout:

- Moodiness or anger
- Defiance
- Anxiety and stress
- Fatigue and chronic pain
- Insomnia
- Withdrawal
- Deteriorating performance and a feeling that one has "peaked"
- Lack of enjoyment, feeling stale
- Boredom
- Loss of idealism and purpose

I have noticed that some children are more prone to burnout than others. Highly susceptible children are often very accomplished in what they do. Their parents, teachers, and coaches (either in agreement with the children or without their acquiescence) set high, sometimes unrealistic goals, such as Olympic gold, when these children are very young. High achievers tend to invest a great deal of time and effort trying to meet the expectations of others. They usually don't react well or are hypersensitive to criticism; they may have a brittle support system. They will often suffer from boredom if the training regimen is too repetitive. These traits cause many highly talented people to lose interest before reaching their potential and indeed are sometimes used by elite coaches to sort the highly focused, perfectionist, resilient winning wheat from the chaff.

If you recognize signs of burnout in your child, don't wait for the "phase" to pass. Encourage your child to talk about his feelings, recognizing that children are often hesitant to admit that they no longer enjoy their special activity. They are especially afraid of disappointing or angering parents caught up in ABPD traps. "I'm forcing you to do it for your own good" or "We've invested far too much money to pull out now" are typical comments from such ABPD parents. Assure your child that you will love and support him whether or not he continues to develop his talent at the current level of intensity, even allowing that you as an adult and parent may feel real disappointment. This is a disappointment that you as a mature adult can deal with.

Many cases of burnout can be resolved by offering the child a change of pace. Consider these ideas:

- Take a break for a while: vary the schedule, include different activities, develop different skills, use different types of thinking, and tap different fields of creativity.
- Find a new instructor.
- Arrange a schedule that is less demanding and requires less sacrifice at this time.

In Sara's case, when her parents sympathized with her feelings and suggested she stop her lessons and performances for a while, Sara was shocked. "I thought you'd be so angry if I didn't play the piano," she confessed. After a full week of staying away from the piano (during which time her parents continued to show support and clear, noncontingent love), Sara asked if she could start her lessons again. Apparently Sara had thought that playing the piano was something she *had* to do. Giving her the freedom to reframe her dilemma and choose for herself, without parental repercussions, allowed her to rekindle her inner flame and personal motivation for working hard with pleasure.

I have seen it happen over and over again: kids who feel trapped by parental expectations are ripe for burnout. Although not all cases will resolve themselves as nicely as Sara's, all signs of burnout need to be recognized and reviewed. If a child's sense of burnout is allowed to continue for a longer period of time, you will see the symptoms rapidly escalate into the more harmful and dangerous manifestations and behaviors discussed later in this chapter.

I Need a Break!

"Usually once a year, we'll see a dancer at the School of American Ballet who is struggling with the program and is very unhappy. He or she may miss home or miss being a typical kid, or may realize that the internal drive just isn't there. But the pressure to succeed is so great sometimes that kids in this situation just can't bring themselves to say so and will begin to act out by breaking rules or falling behind in their work so they can be asked to leave. They'll plead to stay but once their bags are packed you can see that there's a great sense of relief.

"When a child who is talented in the performing arts begins to act up behaviorally or seems to be struggling to keep up, parents have to look at themselves to see what messages they've been giving their child. I don't like to use the term *stage parents,* but there are parents who try to control their child's destiny. Parents have to look at what kind of expectations and pressures they're putting on their child. They should always let their kids know it's OK to take a break or to try other things."

Peter Libman, director of student life, School of
American Ballet, New York City

Overtraining

Overtraining in athletics or the performing arts defeats the purpose of physical conditioning. Children who endure long, tortuous practices and workouts do not necessarily become stronger or tougher. They actually become more prone to acute and chronic injury, which can be both debilitating and career ending. When the stress on the developing young body is too great, breakdowns occur. Overtraining has ruined the elbows of many young pitchers, the knees of young dancers, the shoulders of young golfers, and the wrists of young gymnasts. The continuous stress put on developing ligaments, tendons, joints, and flexible, cartilaginous spines can simply be too much to bear. Orthopedic surgeons, such as Lyle Micheli of Boston Children's Hospital, are noting a rise in such injuries directly related to strenuous, repetitious training activities that seem to be in vogue among elite performers and athletes who focus on only one activity all year long.

As your child trains, watch for these signs of overtraining, which can overlap with the signs and symptoms of burnout:

- Feelings of extreme tiredness and listlessness during workouts
- Chronic sensation of fatigue even away from the gym or practice room
- Prolonged soreness in the joints, bones (caused by shin splints or stress fractures), tendons, and muscle groups or "compartments"
- Insomnia
- Irritability
- Decreased interest in performance

> The number of kids who are being treated for overuse injuries—slow-building stress fractures, for example, or chronic muscle tears that come from throwing too many passes or pitches—is skyrocketing, says Rita Glassman, spokeswoman for the National Youth Sports Safety Foundation in Boston. In fact, she says these injuries are occurring in "epidemic proportion" (Gold and Weber, 2000, p. A1).

- Reduced speed, strength, and endurance
- Slower reflexes

These symptoms can appear at any level of performance when children are pushed beyond their physical capabilities. In ABPD situations where the Nietzchean motto "What doesn't kill me makes me stronger" rules, they are routinely ignored even by professionals who should know better.

In supportive homes, when parents sensitively notice signs of overtraining, they immediately step in to help the child recover before the fatigued body becomes injured. You can do this by

- Allowing one to two days off from training.
- Having your child engage in relaxing activities, such as recreational play (active rest), warm baths, and massage.
- Getting an independent orthopedic evaluation, including X rays or other imaging, if necessary, to rule out stress fractures.
- Arranging for independent physical therapy or occupational therapy assessments if needed.
- Checking the child's diet for proper nutritional intake. Routine blood and urine workups may reveal signs of chronic anemia, or bacterial or viral infection, or immune deficiency.

Be sure to talk to the child's instructor (who is your and your child's employee in a sense) about signs of overtraining and burnout. This person may not be aware that the workouts are too strenuous for your child. If the instructor doesn't plan to change the practice

The Hurried Child

"If we can overcome some of the stresses of our adult lives and decenter, we begin to appreciate the value of childhood with its own special joys, sorrows, worries, and rewards. Valuing childhood does not mean seeing it as a happy innocent period but, rather, as an important period of life to which children are entitled. It is children's right to be children. In the end, a childhood is the most basic human right of children" (Elkind, 1989, p. 202).

regimen to avoid injury, this is when parents who are not beholden to ABPD traps find a new and more astute instructor.

Depression

When children and adolescents seem sad, it is often chalked off as a passing case of the blues. When the sadness persists, these children are labeled as sulky or sensitive and encouraged to "perk up." Many of these kids are actually suffering from undiagnosed cases of low-grade depression, also known as dysthymia, or major depression. Depression is a treatable illness in which feelings of sadness persist and interfere with a child's or adolescent's ability to function. I can't emphasize enough that because children under chronic stress are especially vulnerable, parents of high-achieving children need to be vigilant to the signs and symptoms of depression.

You should suspect depression if you notice one or more of the following signs for more than a couple of weeks:

- Persistent sad, anxious, or "empty" mood
- Loss of interest in activities that previously brought great pleasure and fun
- Feelings of hopelessness, pessimism
- Feelings of guilt, worthlessness, helplessness
- Sleep disturbances (insomnia, early morning waking, or oversleeping)
- Eating disturbances (loss of appetite and weight, or weight gain)
- Decreased energy, fatigue, being "slowed down"
- Restlessness, irritability
- Difficulty concentrating, remembering, and making decisions

Early diagnosis and medical treatment are essential for depressed children. This is a real illness that requires professional help. Comprehensive biopsychosocial treatment often includes individual and family therapy. It may also include the use of antidepressant medication. For more comprehensive help, parents should ask their physician to refer them to a child and adolescent psychiatrist who can diagnose and treat depression and other conditions, such as the mixed high and low bipolar affective and anxiety disorders.

Suicide Watch

A depressed child is at increased risk for committing suicide and homicide, as well-publicized cases in schools across America show. Although parents may wonder why a child with her whole wonderful life in front of her would even consider causing her own death, the fact is that suicide is the third leading cause of death for fifteen- to twenty-four-year-olds and the sixth leading cause of death for five- to fourteen-year-olds (American Academy of Child and Adolescent Psychiatry, 1998). In high-achieving children, who are often stressed and pressured, it is something to be aware of and to look out for.

Many of the symptoms of suicidal feelings are similar to those of depression. In addition, a teen who is planning to commit suicide may also

- Complain of being a bad person or feeling "rotten inside"
- Describe hearing voices telling him to hurt himself
- Give hints by saying such things as "I won't bother you much longer," "Nothing matters anyway," "It's no use," and "I won't see you again"
- Put her affairs in order—for example, give away favorite possessions, clean her room, throw away important belongings, write a farewell letter or suicide note, or make out a will
- Become suddenly cheerful after a period of depression
- Demonstrate a powerful, driven anxiety to "finish things"
- Have a family history of suicide, depression, manic-depressive or bipolar illness, or suicide
- Be male (male teenagers complete suicide at a higher rate than females, who attempt suicide more frequently)
- Be abusing alcohol or drugs, which further impairs judgment

Asking the child whether he is depressed or thinking about suicide can be helpful. In my profession it is standard to talk openly but very sensitively about suicide with people suffering depression. I might ask, "Have you ever thought about hurting or even killing yourself? Have you ever made plans for it or actually attempted it? How would you go about doing it? Do you have the [gun, knife, poison, pills, suicide note] ready?" You may be afraid of these questions. Rather than "putting thoughts in the child's head," such questions provide assurance that somebody cares, is aware, and will give the young person a safety valve—the chance to talk about problems that sometimes seem insoluble.

If any of these signs occur, parents need to talk to their child about their concerns and seek emergency professional help. With support from family and with professional treatment, children who are suicidal can heal and safely return to a healthier lifestyle and developmental path.

Psychosomatic Pain and Illness

Psychosomatic pain and illness syndromes are suspected when, despite appropriate treatment, relatively minor illnesses (such as stomachaches) and the pain of injuries (such as a sprained ankle or tendonitis of the ankle, knee, or shoulder) persist. The child will continue to complain of severe discomfort and will be unable to return to her athletic, academic, or performing art training even when medically cleared to do so. Not surprisingly, when these children can no longer hide behind the medical problem and must return to active participation, they are very likely to suffer another illness or injury. After a history of minor medical problems, they may progress to overt self-destructive behavior to sustain a major debilitating injury or illness. Physicians have noticed a growing trend of psychologically mediated pain and illness syndromes in child and adolescent elite-level performers.

The following are four types of psychosomatic syndromes that I have seen in my practice with high-achieving children. You should consider them a possible cause if physical ailments frequently keep your child from performing or competing.

Malingering

This syndrome occurs when a child hurts herself deliberately to achieve a certain goal—typically an excuse to stop performing or competing. Children and adolescents have been known to intentionally sprain ankles or burn or cut themselves to end the perceived torture of endless high-level training.

What happened to a figure skater we'll call Jane is a perfect example. Jane, who is twelve years old, has been training six days a week (including vacations) for the past three years after her parents (her father in particular) decided that she had the ability to become an Olympic competitor. At first Jane loved the sport, but into her third year, her interest was flagging. She began to "sleep in" early mornings when she was due to attend practice. She began, like her school friends, to become more interested in boys. She also began to menstruate and to grow taller. She found that she wasn't as graceful on the ice as she had been, and her coach became more impatient and demanding.

Jane's mother, who had attended every practice in those long years, was also not particularly sympathetic. She felt that Jane was on the cusp of developing certain skills necessary to "make the big leap" to the big time. She wanted her daughter to hang in there to reap the rewards of their mutual sacrifices. But one morning, Jane decided that she had had enough. She found the courage to tell her parents and her coach that she wanted to quit. They all refused in dismissive patronizing fashion to listen to her "nonsense" and went on arranging for her next competition as if she hadn't said a word.

Jane was desperate; she decided to write her own ticket to freedom. She threw herself into a very difficult spin too close to the barriers, where she hit her leg and sustained a simple fracture of the tibia. She was forced to be in a cast for two months. She had found a win-win way of getting out of skating. Her parents and coach were perversely proud of the aggressive bravery she showed in attempting such a difficult move, and she had a ready-made reason for forced retirement and for resuming a more normal life like that of her friends.

Unfortunately, malingering is only a temporary solution until the injury heals. For this reason, shortly after they heal, children who choose this route to saving face and saving their sanity will often find another creative way of getting injured or not being able to train or compete.

Factitious Illness

In factitious illness, the child feigns sickness so that he can be excused from a dreaded activity and at the same time gain the support and sympathy of caretakers, family, and instructors. It is the extreme example of the stomachache that schoolchildren pretend to have on the morning of the big test.

Jimmy, for example, is a fifteen-year-old math whiz. He is on the fast track to a prestigious university, with straight A's in advanced placement college-prep courses. He is also attending weekend classes at the local college. His parents, who are both engineers, are very proud of him and often brag to their friends and colleagues about his academic accomplishments. Jimmy is getting very tired of studying late into every night, but he feels that his high grades are the only thing that gain him his parents' love and attention. He has no close friends and very few social contacts to turn to. He desperately needs a break, but he can't risk disappointing his parents and losing their support. Then he sees a TV drama about an emergency appendectomy and gets an idea.

Jimmy begins to complain about pain in his lower left abdomen and makes himself vomit several times. His parents are very fearful, and they take him straight to the emergency room of the local hospital, where the surgery residents feel that, despite the normal lab results, they should remove his appendix. This is kind of scary for Jimmy, but somehow he can't resist the attention he's getting. The nurses attend to his every whim, his classmates send him get-well cards, and his room is filled with balloons and gifts from his family. His mother stays at his side and gives him warm, loving hugs.

A few days later, Jimmy returns home to his studies, and he begins to feel lonely and anxious again. The sympathy of his family is beginning to wane, and his parents push Jimmy to make up the schoolwork he has missed and study hard to catch up. He says he has agonizing pain in the area of his abdominal scar; his dubious parents only half believe this but take him back to the clinic. His doctor sends him back to the emergency room, where he is again admitted by a surgical team who are scratching their heads trying to figure out what has gone wrong. During three days of observation, Jimmy continues to complain bitterly of pain under the scar, heats the thermometer to fake a high temperature, and begs for more and more painkillers (which give him a comforting feeling of being "out of it"). The surgeons then take him back to the operating room, where they find nothing wrong. He begins vomiting when fluids are reintroduced and regains the sympathy and attention of his caregivers and family.

Jimmy may seem like a conniving sneak who is making his family go through hell for nothing, but in fact his behavior is a maladaptive expression of ABPD. Jimmy's need for supportive nurturing aside from his academic accomplishments is so great that he is willing to undergo unnecessary surgery to get it. This child and others like him need parents who freely give support and love that is not conditionally linked to the need for great accomplishment, which in this case the child is just not developmentally prepared for.

Hypochondriasis

Hypochondriasis is a state in which a person is preoccupied with the idea that she suffers from a serious medical ailment, although her assumption is based on a misinterpretation or exaggeration of real but usually minor physical symptoms. The pain and the discomfort are very real, but the cause is psychological. This is analogous to the morning stomachaches that children really do suffer when they're worried about taking a test at school.

A study by Pillemer and Micheli analyzed a case of possible hypochondriasis in sixteen-year-old Julie, who was admitted four times in one month to Children's Hospital in Boston for severe pain in her right foot. Julie had been an avid athlete who participated in her school's gymnastics and track programs. One year before her hospital admissions, Julie had hurt her foot in gym class. The injury was described as a relatively minor sprain that healed well with supportive bandaging and weight-bearing restrictions. When Julie continued to complain of pain, her doctor prescribed a variety of therapeutic measures including exercises and whirlpool massage. The pain continued, so Julie's doctor suggested a psychological assessment to determine if emotional problems might be contributing to her pain. It was found that Julie's injury had occurred at the same time she had begun to lose athletic contests. She eventually admitted that her injury gave her medical protection from pressure to fulfill the expectations of family and friends to rejoin her sports teams (Pillemer and Micheli, 1988).

Not unlike the malingering and factitious examples, children will experience anxiety-related hypochondriasis when they desperately need an escape route from the pressure of performance expectations. Julie's psychological need to avoid the shame of losing did indeed cause her to experience real pain.

Conversion Disorder (Hysterical Illness)

A conversion disorder is an unconsciously produced symptom or deficit that affects voluntary movement or sensation. People experiencing this psychosomatic problem usually gain some benefit in their lives through the paralysis or loss of function of some part of their body.

John, for example, is a sixteen-year-old who had been excelling in all subjects at school as well as at soccer, which he had been playing competitively since age ten as a goalkeeper. His father is very anxious for John to get a soccer scholarship and go to college to study engineering like his older brother. Dad is a stiff-upper-lip parent and will not tolerate anything less than the best from his children, both in school and on the playing fields.

One year ago, John's best friend and co-goalie, who had shared fifty-fifty goalie time for the team, was killed in a car accident. John's father's reaction to the death was to say, "Oh well, now you better get on with it; it's sad, but there's nothing we can do now. Actually, there's a silver lining because now you'll be able to play every game!"

John was not able to sleep well. His grades and his soccer performance fell off. Eventually, John collapsed at soccer practice, experiencing facial twitching and shaking in both arms. He was admitted to hospital for a seizure workup, but his EEG and neurological testing all came up normal.

After a two-hour session with a psychiatrist, John confessed his feelings of guilt about benefiting from the death of his best friend and his fear of disappointing his father now that he was the team's only goalie. With some cognitive therapy and antianxiety medication, John's symptoms slowly began to resolve. Family therapy over the next few months focused on increasing communication within the family, enabling John to be more assertive in expressing his feelings, allowing his father to "lighten up" a little and be more tolerant of normal grief and the stress of high school for his son, and permitting John's mother to become a little more assertive in expressing her own feelings in the household.

Several months later, John is still experiencing occasional facial twitching and arm weakness, but he is now able to perform well in both school and in soccer. He is much happier with his life, his realistic college plans, and his family relationships.

If your child suffers recurring illnesses, pain, or injuries that his doctor can't explain and that prohibit him from practicing, studying, or performing, a psychosomatic pain or illness syndrome may be the explanation. Your reaction to this situation is crucial to your child's recovery. ABPD parents are known to become angry or intolerant in this situation. They can't imagine why a high achiever would want to be sidelined. Either they go from doctor to doctor looking for one who can find a physical reason for the problem, or they blame the child for "lying" and push him back into the spotlight. Supportive parents, in contrast, ask their doctors for advice on finding competent psychological counseling with someone trained to recognize and work with these psychological and physiologic manifestations of excessive pressure.

Eating Disorders

Eating disorders seem to cluster among high-achieving children. Individuals most prone to disorders such as anorexia nervosa and bulimia are usually bright, artistic, and self-disciplined females between the ages of twelve and twenty-five. It is believed that these girls are very anxious to please their parents, teachers, and coaches, and they continually strive for perfection. It's no wonder high-achieving kids are the hardest hit.

Case Study

Researchers Marks and Goldberg evaluated twenty-five athletes who were sent to them for a second opinion regarding severe incapacitating pain following orthopedic injuries that are usually minimally distressing. Intensive medical and imaging work-ups confirmed the original diagnosis in all twenty-five cases; in all the cases the researchers also diagnosed an adjustment disorder in which the patient experienced disproportionate pain unconsciously motivated by the need to escape the pressure associated with sports participation. This underlines the need for psychological consultation during the injury and rehabilitation process (Stryer, Tofler, and Lapchick, 1998).

Anorexia Nervosa and Bulimia

The most common eating disorders found in children are anorexia nervosa and bulimia. Anorexia nervosa is essentially self-starvation; bulimia involves binge eating and purging—that is, consuming large, high-calorie meals and vomiting or taking laxatives (or both) in an attempt to expel the food before it can be absorbed by the body. Either problem may include a number of pathogenic weight-control behaviors, such as

- Extreme dieting
- Vomiting
- Abuse of laxatives
- Abuse of diuretics
- Extreme exercise

Although certainly not limited to one activity or sport, weight-reduction disorders are more likely to affect gymnasts, figure skaters, swimmers, models, dancers, and runners, whose performances are compromised by excess fat and are driven by aesthetic considerations. In the general population, an astounding estimated 15 percent of young women have substantially disordered eating attitudes and behaviors, but this number skyrockets among elite performers and athletes. The prevalence of at least one pathogenic weight-control behavior jumps among female college gymnasts into the range of 62 percent to 74 percent. Among ballet dancers, the prevalence of anorexia nervosa and bulimia is as high as 25.7 percent and 19 percent respectively. In a group of elite female swimmers from fourteen to thirty years of age, nearly 70 percent of their coaches had instructed them to lose weight (Baum, 1998). The weight-loss tactics of starvation, self-induced vomiting, diet pills, and laxative abuse have become quite common. The frightening reality of this problem is uncovered when we learn that 70 percent of college athletes who use pathogenic weight-control tactics report that they believe their behavior is harmless!

Parents who are not caught up in an ABPD trap make sure their children know that dangerous weight-control tactics are very harmful. Anorexia and bulimia are serious disorders that can keep young scholars, athletes, and performers from reaching their full potential and make them prone to injury and illness. If you're ever tempted to look the other way when you see your child dropping weight to enhance performance, remind yourself of this: the medical consequences of anorexia nervosa include malnutrition, shrunken organs, bone mineral loss (sometimes leading to osteoporosis), low body temperature, low blood pressure, slowed metabolism and reflexes, and irregular heartbeat that sometimes leads to cardiac arrest and death. The medical consequences of bulimia include dehydration; damage to bowels, liver, and kidney; tooth and gum erosion; tears of the esophagus; and electrolyte imbalance that can lead to irregular heartbeat and, in some cases, cardiac arrest and death. Some young women carry these disorders into adulthood, and about 6 percent overall of those with eating disorders die from their complications.

A child's desire to drop weight may be caused by a combination of pressures from coaches, instructors, parents, peers, society, or the media. It's thought that this pressure may actually trigger eating disorders in those with specific vulnerabilities. Sometimes it takes only an offhand remark or an overheard comment about excess weight to trigger the onset of an eating disorder. Consider the case of fifteen-year-old Heather, an attractive, intelligent, and popular track star. Heather's coaches knew she had that extra something that would earn her trophies, championships, and eventually a lucrative college scholarship. As she finished her freshman season, the varsity coach took Heather aside to compliment her talent and to assure her of a place on the varsity team the following year. He also asked her to follow a prescribed off-season conditioning program that would bring her to the field in top shape. The coach half-jokingly called over his shoulder a parting comment: "And stay away from the sweet stuff, Heather. A track star needs to be lean."

With the enthusiasm of an Olympic hopeful, Heather immediately threw herself into the suggested program of exercises and put herself on a strict reducing diet. After two weeks, however, Heather still felt out of shape and fat. She doubled her daily exercise time and decided to eat nothing but two apples a day until she had a "lean" body. Several months later, weak and emaciated and with self-induced scratches and cuts, Heather was hospitalized and fed against her will intravenously. Once in top shape and perfect health, Heather was now unable to walk even a few feet without suffering total exhaustion; she was suffering from anorexia nervosa, and her parents hadn't a clue. They figured that all teens go through fad diets, and they felt that if the coach wanted her to lose weight in order to compete for a place on the varsity team and maybe a scholarship, he must know what he's talking about.

Heather's eating disorder took her family by surprise. They all had their eye on the target of improved performance and weren't looking for the signs and symptoms of trouble. Be sure to read the

Warning Signs of Anorexia Nervosa

- Loss of significant amount of weight
- Continuous dieting, even when thin
- Intense fear of gaining weight
- Compulsive exercise
- Absent or irregular menstruation
- Hair loss
- Ritualistic eating behavior, such as organizing food on a plate or dawdling over food

Warning Signs of Bulimia

- Binge eating, usually in secret
- Purging by strict dieting, fasting, vigorous exercise, vomiting, or abusing laxatives or diuretics
- Using the bathroom frequently after meals
- Compulsive exercise
- Swollen salivary glands
- Bloodshot eyes
- A persistent sore throat from constant vomiting
- Dehydration and dry skin
- Abdominal bloating
- Tooth decay caused by inadequate nutrition and frequent vomiting
- Muscle spasms, kidney problems, or cardiac arrest brought on by an electrolyte imbalance caused by loss of body fluids

list of warning signs posted in the box so that you don't miss the red flags of an eating disorder in your child.

Not for Females Only

Although females are more commonly affected by eating disorders, statistics show that males are not exempt. The number of instances of anorexia and bulimia is increasing in young males. This can be seen especially in such sports as wrestling and rowing, which emphasize weight reduction to gain competitive advantage. In a study of 125 high school wrestlers, researchers found that the sample used pathogenic weight-control measures as follows: fasting, 51 percent; diet pills, 14 percent; diuretics, 10 percent; laxatives, 8 percent; and vomiting, 15 percent (Weissinger and others, 1991). These are disturbing numbers.

Unhealthy weight reduction is not something that can be ignored because "everybody" does it. There is evidence that food restriction and weight loss, if followed by a return to initial weight levels, results in a lower metabolic rate, making future weight loss more difficult. Children who repeatedly lose weight for competitions and then gain it back are setting themselves up for lifelong weight battles. Rapid weight loss has other negative consequences as well. Fluid restriction and dehydration through the use of saunas, rubber suits, diuretics, laxatives, self-induced vomiting, and exercise can have deadly consequences. The electrolyte disturbances caused by fluid loss can increase the risk of cardiac arrhythmia, renal damage, impaired performance, and injuries. They also can influence cardiac output and core temperature, which may have dangerous consequences. Competing in this compromised physical state is likely to cause not only fatigue and poor physical performance but also injury or even death.

Wrestlers are most notorious for using dangerous weight-loss practices, but any sport where weight is a consideration is open to abuse. A local mother tells us of her surprise when she arrived early to pick up her ten-year-old son from a preseason football practice. "I found him wrapped in large plastic bags, sitting in the coach's car with the windows rolled up and the heater on full blast!" The coach explained that her son was over the weight limit for this team and that if he didn't lose seven pounds by Saturday, he would not be allowed to play for the entire season. Should this family let their son sweat, dehydrate, starve, and risk serious illness for a week, or should they yank him from that sauna on wheels and never return?

The family's decision will depend on how they feel about their son playing football. If they are caught in an ABPD trap that puts their own enthusiasm for the game or their own hopes of glory in their son's accomplishments out front, it will be very difficult for them to put his health first.

Confronting an Eating Disorder

Distorted eating patterns are not necessarily caused by ABPD, but the parental response to the problem is dictated by their freedom from or entanglement in ABPD traps. Those who are struggling with meeting their own needs through their children will ignore or deny the danger of eating problems. These parents see the red flags, but because of their own agenda they don't react, and too often they are supported in that position. Denial of eating disorders and pathogenic eating behaviors is often encountered among major sports organizations, educational institutions, and individual coaches and agents who promote athletes and performers. Sadly, refusal to address these problems can impede the diagnosis and treatment of these young people, who may be in serious, and sometimes life-threatening, condition both physically and emotionally.

Supportive parents who see that their child is using dangerous weight-control methods won't let things slide. They know that, regardless of what instructors or teammates may say, there is substantial medical evidence to support the position that children should never lose weight beyond healthy body composition in order to participate or compete in any activity.

If you suspect your child is involved in distorted eating or weight loss behaviors that she is hiding from you, you must confront the issue.

- Tell your child what you see, and express your concern.
- Be empathic but direct.
- Listen carefully to your child's response.
- Don't back down if she initially denies the problem.
- If the situation has become compulsive and no longer under

your child's control, seek professional help, a support group, or both. You can contact psychologists, social workers, or psychiatrists listed in your phone book or recommended by your family doctor. Ask specifically about their experience with treating eating disorders. Ask for a thorough description of their treatment method. Ask how successful their treatment plan has been and what the average length of treatment is.

Substance Abuse

Drug abuse is widespread among adolescents of all levels of achievement and socioeconomic class. Freely available legal drugs frequently abused by many adolescents include alcohol; nicotine in its many forms; prescribed medications; inhalants (glues, aerosols, and solvents); and over-the-counter cough, cold, sleep, and diet medications. Illegal drugs of choice include marijuana; stimulants (cocaine in its different forms, methamphetamine, "ice" (dextroamphetamine); hallucinogens, such as LSD, PCP, or the so-called designer drug MDMA (Ecstasy); opiates, such as heroin or methadone; and steroids and other drugs that enhance performance or power.

Help for Eating Disorders

For more information about eating disorders, contact your doctor or one of the following organizations:

National Association of Anorexia Nervosa
and Associated Disorders
P.O. Box 7
Highland Park, IL 60035
Telephone: (847) 831-3438
Web: www.anad.org.

American Anorexia Bulimia Association, Inc.
165 West 46th Street, Suite 108
New York, NY 10036
Telephone: (212) 575-6200
Web:www.aabainc.org.

Some exceptional kids are at high risk for substance abuse. This group includes those with pre-existing genetic risk factors, those suffering chronic stress, bipolar individuals (manic-depressives who often show powerful creative ability) or others experiencing mood disorders, those who feel they are socially isolated "misfits," those who feel overly pressured to achieve with no sense that there is a viable way out, and those who feel compelled to use drugs for performance enhancement.

Mind-altering substances can "medicate the world away" or at least dull the pain for a little while. They give developing, awkwardly precocious kids the comfort of euphoria and bravado, and the distance and space that they cannot feel in their daily grind. They offer a way to rebel against overly controlling parents, mentors, and coaches who have been pushing them too hard for too long. Substance abuse is among the few activities (along with sex, rock and roll, and fashion) in which they can participate without their parents dictating every move.

The problem of substance abuse among high achievers can be compounded by the parental reaction to this situation. ABPD parents may be afraid that voicing their suspicions will anger their ever-so-special child and interrupt his ability to function on a high level. They may worry that their child will lose his advantage in the classroom, on the playing field, or on the stage if the abuse problem becomes public knowledge (not to mention the embarrassment to the family!). There is also the concern that the child will lose his competitive edge if they believe the substance is the secret formula to the child's success. These parents will ignore or deny the situation as long as the child's performance remains exceptional. Like all adults, ABPD parents may be substance abusers themselves—another reason for ignoring their child's behavior.

Supportive parents who can free themselves from reputation and performance issues will not shy away from the often painful subject of substance abuse. Even high-achieving children (and maybe these children especially) need their parents to talk to them about drug use and tell them about the dangers. They need to know that drug use is associated with increased risk of serious drug use later in life, school dropout and failure, and impaired judgment, all of which put teens at risk for accidents, violence, and unplanned and unsafe sex and all its complications, from pregnancy to STDs. Research has repeatedly shown that parental communication, early and often, is the single most important factor in preventing kids from using drugs.

If a high-achieving child becomes involved in substance abuse and begins to fall off the ladder of success, ABPD parents react strongly. A distancing, objectifying parent may use rationalizations we have mentioned before, including minimization, pseudoautonomy, or plausible deniability—to place the blame squarely on the shoulders of the "adultified" child and avoid looking at underlying precipitating stressors. Other parents, especially those who are controlling and highly involved, react with narcissistic rage or anger. The substance abuse is risking destruction of their own dreams of fortune and fame. Because they are unable to focus on the needs of the child as separate from (or even greater than) their own needs, the ABPD parent falls back on strategies that worked well (from a developmental standpoint) for the adult-pleasing latency-aged ten-year-old. But as demands for obedience, practice, and top performance increase, the newly oppositional, twelve- or thirteen-year-old defiant and independent-minded adolescent can become more involved in self-destructive behavior.

Responsible and alert parents are keenly aware of the signs of drug use (without being overly intrusive). These include rolling papers, pipes, and matches; empty aerosol spray cans (from "huffing" or inhaling fumes); the strong smell of glue, solvents, or liquid correction fluid in the bedroom; soda cans that have been dented and poked with holes (used as smoking devices); plastic bags in the bedroom (commonly used to store drugs); or saline eye drops (to get the pot-induced red out). These are red flags that can't be ignored, even by parents who have intelligent, apparently responsible, exceptional kids.

The Problem with Steroids and Other Performance-Enhancing Drugs

The use of performance-enhancing drugs has become a family affair in many circles and is tacitly ignored, if not directly encouraged, by parents and involved adults who hope to give their young future stars the competitive edge. Athletes frequently gain a real, but double-edged, advantage through the use of anabolic steroids and synthetic hormones that promote the growth of muscle tissue (and hence power) and enhance recovery after workouts and injury. Although these drugs are banned in most sports and are in some cases illegal, athletes still use them to gain significant increases in strength and lean body mass relative to those that would occur from training alone. (In fact, steroids could ironically symbolize the Olympic motto: *higher, faster, stronger.*) Steroid use has moved beyond body building, wrestling, and professional sports such as football and baseball. It is now a problem affecting many adolescents competing in local high school arenas. The societal values related to the importance of sports, winning, college scholarships, and physical appearance strongly influence this demand.

Seventeen-year-old Rick is a powerful linebacker on the varsity football team. His exceptional speed, muscular strength, and size have the college recruiters drooling. Rick and his dad, who coached him until recently, tell their friends that his sudden jump in athletic accomplishment is due to a rigorous off-season weight-training program. Deep down, Rick's dad knows better. He's noticed that Rick hasn't grown in height at all in the last year. He's watched his son's mild-mannered personality change into a short-tempered volatile one. He's noticed that Rick's facial hair is exceptionally thick and that he's using it to cover up his acne. Rick's dad knows that the large muscles, growth cessation, the sudden and dramatic change to a more explosive personality, heavy facial hair, and acne all point to steroid use, but Dad has remained quiet. If "everyone" else is

Young Abusers

The 1995 Youth Risk and Behavior Surveillance System data showed that of ninth to twelfth graders in public and private high schools in the United States, 4.9 percent of boys and 2.4 percent of girls have used anabolic steroids at least once in their lives. This translates to approximately 375,000 adolescent male and 175,000 adolescent female steroid users (Kann and others, 1996). In addition to these numbers, it has been reported that 7 percent of steroid users started using the drug at ten years of age or younger (Gaa and others, 1994).

using steroids to get into college programs, why shouldn't his son level the playing field?

This is the line of reasoning that gets kids like Rick involved with performance-enhancing drugs in the first place. Both male and female athletics place great emphasis on body composition, weight, and appearance. In highly competitive, so-called elite environments, athletes are sometimes tempted to alter their physical makeup and size to improve their performance, impress their peers, please their coaches and parents, and give them an advantage over their opponents (or, at the very least, prevent a qualitative disadvantage). They see others taking steroids in pill form or by injection, and they see only the quick, positive effects: an aggressive and vigorous attitude, larger muscle size in less training time, and increased amounts of energy and speed.

What they don't see immediately are the negative body changes that steroid abuse can cause down the pike. One such change actually *causes* sports-related injuries. It has been found that some users experience an increased risk of injury to muscles, tendons, and ligaments. Steroids do not strengthen the muscle supports. When muscles get too bulky for their supports, they are prone to injury, and they then do not heal as well or as quickly as they would had they developed naturally.

Steroids also have a negative effect on many functions of the body and the brain, including the male testes and the female reproductive organs. In males, this can decrease sperm production and cause a reduction in the size of the testes. These effects can lead to testicular cancer, infertility, sterility, or all three. Male athletes may also develop female-like breast tissue. These side effects may occur temporarily during the period of steroid use, or they may become permanent conditions.

Females who abuse steroids may notice the development of male-pattern baldness, growth of facial and body hair, deepening of the voice, coarsening of the features, and a decrease in breast size. Unfortunately for the female, most side effects of steroid abuse are irreversible.

In addition to bodily changes, steroid users may also experience psychological problems, such as mood depression, nervous tension, irritability, hostility, aggression, sleep problems, delusions, and even suicidal tendencies. Obviously, steroids are not the innocuous wonder drugs they may at first seem to be. Nevertheless, families stuck in an ABPD bind allow the abuse to continue in exchange for the gold of high achievement.

Parents like Rick's, who can't put the health of their child above their own need to see him rise above the crowd, will minimize the negatives, hide behind misinformation, deny, ignore, or blatantly encourage steroid use and abuse. But those who see their children as more than mere "producers" will make sure their high-achieving kids know about the dangers of steroid use. They will tell them that

- There are many negative short- and long-term medical consequences of steroid abuse.
- As soon as the user stops taking the drugs, the extra weight and muscle mass are quickly lost, but many of the negative effects stay behind.
- Steroids are psychologically and, to a lesser degree, physically addictive.

The Latest Muscle Builder

Lots of adolescents are trading in steroids for the latest fad in muscle building: androstenedione. It's legal. It's sold over the counter to anyone who wants to buy it. And it's getting lots of media hype. Although it is banned by the Olympics, the NCAA, the NFL, and the men's and women's professional tennis tours, Major League Baseball has not taken a stand on this substance, and its use by high-profile professional athletes, such as St. Louis Cardinals' slugger Mark McGwire, makes it hard for young would-be superstars to resist. At this time, the supplement is unregulated, and long-term health studies have not been completed. But a 2000 study financed by Major League Baseball has uncovered danger signs. The study found that androstenedione increases levels of the male hormone, testosterone, and therefore can cause the same hazardous side effects of steroids. You should talk to your family doctor before allowing a developing child or adolescent to use this body builder (even if "everyone else" is using it).

- Steroid use is cheating: cheating in the sport, cheating fellow athletes, and cheating one's own body.
- College teams don't want athletes whose performance is the result of steroids (which are banned by the NCAA) rather than natural ability.
- You, as a responsible parent, will jump in and run interference to protect your child the moment you feel anything but hard work and effort is behind muscle growth and physical performance.

If you believe your child is trying to gain a performance edge by abusing steroids, androstenedione, creatine, erythropoetin (EPO), growth hormone (GH), or other performance enhancers, discuss your suspicions with your family physician, sports medicine specialist, or sports psychiatrist. Then arrange an opportunity for your child to discuss steroid use with the doctor. The physician can objectively talk about negative side effects, administer a blood test to detect steroid or other drug use, and determine if any steroid-related conditions, such as hypertension or abnormal liver or kidney function, are already present.

Answering a Cry for Help

From burnout to substance abuse to suicide, the effects of ABPD can be devastating to the child, her parents, and her future potential. The red flags discussed in this chapter are examples of the kinds of warning signals or cries for help sent out by high achievers under stress. Keep your eyes open and respond to any warning signs quickly, because it is the health of your child that really should be your top priority. Fame, glory, accomplishment, and financial rewards do have their place, but not at the ultimate risk to sound physical and mental health. Without them our children cannot reap any of the rewards of success.

Step Seven

Take a Good Look at Your Parenting Style

The last step in encouraging and protecting athletes, scholars, and performing artists is one that requires a willingness on your part to do a tough but honest self-evaluation that will be beneficial to both you and your child. This chapter will ask you to look at your own role in your child's development and determine if you have crossed over the line from normal and supportive parenting to the dangerous area of Achievement by Proxy Distortion (ABPD). Remember also to evaluate the parenting style of your spouse. As a parent and guardian of your child, you are equally responsible for any ABPD behaviors your spouse may be involved in, and you must act to prevent the results of abusive ABPD.

There are many reasons that parents struggle with ABPD. The ones we discuss in the next sections will give you an overview of the most common roots of trouble. A parent may easily get caught up in any one or in several at a time. The key is to recognize them if they exist in your family. Surely we all know parents like the ones in this book who look the other way when an instructor verbally or even physically hurts their child. We know parents who insist that their child give up or severely curtail all socializing in order to spend more time practicing or studying, who dictate every movement the child makes, who bully, prod, and push the child to the top, who ignore illness or injury for the sake of continued performance. We can recognize these other parents and even identify their motives. They might do these things because they are autocratic, narcissistic, greedy, overly competitive, frustrated by their own thwarted dreams, or in frank denial.

But are we as clear sighted in our relationship with our own children? Can we recognize when we or our spouses are making decisions for our children based solely on our own needs rather than theirs? Can we see ourselves moving rapidly through the three stages of ABPD: risky sacrifice, objectification, and abuse? It takes an honest self-analysis to answer these questions, but in the end, honest answers can save a family and a child from years of unhappiness, heartache, and blame.

At the end of each section is a short self-analysis questionnaire. If you find yourself answering yes to more than one or two of the "red flag" questions in any one section, you might be an ABPD parent who needs to spend more time focusing on your child's real developmental needs, goals, and dreams and less on your own.

Autocratic Controller

Autocratic parents rule their children with a firm will—and sometimes the back of their hand. They are usually overly involved in their children's lives and have the unshakable belief that they know what is best, regardless of how the child feels. Autocratic parents have their eye on the prize, and nothing the child says or does will change the decisions they make regarding the child's training and upbringing. They need to be in complete control. These parents often have run-ins with the child's instructors, whom they resent for having influence over their children. They know best, and nobody else can tell them how to develop the child's talent. (For this reason, their children often are homeschooled, where they cannot be exposed to dangerous outside ideas.) As we have previously explained, sometimes, autocratic parents are the previously described infamous, caricatured stage mothers and sports parents who stand on the sidelines screaming, cursing, ridiculing, and demeaning every wrong move their child makes. In other situations, they can be much more subtle and surreptitious in their destructive behavior toward their children. The undermining can be quietly cutting and equally hostile in private. These parents may, for example, be dictating a child's rituals and eating behaviors down to the exact calorie at home and be severely limiting social contacts depending on the child's performance level. They are aggressively overly determined parents whose driving anger and controlling natures can be loud or mute.

Other chapters in this book have told stories of autocratic parents and their high achievers. There was Janine in Step Five, whose grades began to fall when she suffered terrible headaches every time a test was scheduled. Her parents ignored her tears and told her to stop whining and take the test. When this didn't solve the problem, they scolded her for having headaches "for no good reason" and for her dropping grades.

There was Jane, the figure skater in Step Six, who created an excuse to quit her grueling practice schedule by intentionally breaking her leg. If you remember, Jane told her mother that she wanted to quit, but her mother "refused in dismissive patronizing fashion to listen to her 'nonsense' and went on arranging for her next competition."

In "From Benign to Abusive" in Part One, you heard about the successful pianist Ruth Slenczynska, whose autocratic father slapped and shoved her when she made a mistake during her piano practice. He decided that "[n]ot a moment of her life was to be 'wasted' in playing with dolls, skipping rope, going to a movie, riding a tricycle, or playing with other children."

You might also remember the story of the math scholar, Donna, in Step Two. The actions of her autocratic father show us how this type of parent can easily progress through the stages of ABPD: Donna's father decided, without consulting his wife or Donna, that his daughter would leave her neighborhood school and enroll in the Academy of Math and Science. Then he had her skip algebra in her freshman year and move right to geometry. These were risky sacrifices that might or might not pay off for Donna.

When Donna's father heard that she was not placed in honors geometry, he demanded, over the rational and supportive objections of her teachers, that she be moved into the higher-level class. Here Donna's father was objectifying her. Donna was being pressured to perform to satisfy her father's demands. Her father was not merely failing to consider Donna's feelings, abilities, and developmental capabilities—he was blatantly ignoring them.

Finally, when Donna's grades did not meet her father's expectations, he became enraged, in part because his own ambitions were being thwarted. At this point he moved into the potentially abusive range of ABPD. He made his daughter quit the tennis team and enrolled her in precollege mathematics courses at a university. He pushed her to use all her free time studying math. Donna did not have the mathematical ability to meet her father's goals, yet he continued to push her toward something that was very important to him alone. This is a distorted, potentially abusive form of autocratic parenting that takes away all opportunities for socialization and other forms of fun that children have a right to experience. It helps create a one-dimensional human being for the purpose of satisfying the parent's needs.

Are You an Autocratic Controller?

Answer honestly the questions that follow. Every time you think deep down that the answer is yes, this should be a red flag that you may be in the ABPD parent zone.

1. Do you frequently feel that your child's instructors "don't know what they're doing"?
2. Do you not only determine exactly how, when, and how long your child will study or practice but also how she will spend any downtime or play time?
3. Do you frequently criticize your child's performance, hoping to motivate her to work harder?
4. Are you willing to alter your work schedule to be constantly on top of what your child does so that your sacrifices will not be in vain and she can really be the best?
5. Do you make decisions about your child's training without thinking about her age, developmental stage, and capabilities, or without getting some input from the child herself?
6. Do you make plans, arrangements, and commitments for your child that may affect the entire family, without any family discussion or input?

Narcissistic and Needy

Parental pride and pleasure in a child's performance and achievements is 100 percent appropriate, and identifying strongly with his or her child is a part of every parent's life. Extremely narcissistic parents, however, by necessity bask in the reflected glory of their children, which, in a way, is their oxygen. They need their children to be the best so that they themselves can feel admired by others. Their own need for attention and approval drives them to push their children to the top. These are the parents who storm out of an athletic event or an artistic performance when their child makes a mistake. They are embarrassed for themselves, not at all for their child unless as an afterthought. They demand high grades of their scholars because this accomplishment proves to others (and to themselves) that they are good parents.

Throughout this book we have met narcissistic parents, including the autocratic parents who pushed their children for their own gratification. You might remember the baseball player in Step One who made his father extremely proud by earning an athletic scholarship to college, but who then quit the team and was disowned. The father became depressed and refused to talk to his son for several years. This father felt his son had let him down by taking away the one thing that was most important in *his* life. What the boy wanted, even as a young adult, did not matter.

There was also the story in Step Four of Marian, the mother who built her own life around her daughter's enjoyment of theatrical productions. This mother dedicated her time and interest to her child's performance activities. When her daughter was a high school sophomore and decided she'd rather get an after-school job and hang out with her friends than devote her time to stage rehearsals, Marian was utterly lost. She had nothing of her own to be involved in or to be proud of. She had lived in the reflected glow of her daughter's spotlight, and now she had nothing.

You might also remember the story of young John in Step One, whose parents wanted him to be a stage vocalist. When John matured and his voice teacher told his parents that their son was tone deaf and could not progress to higher levels of instruction, they became very personally insulted and angry. They had already entered the first stage of ABPD by making many sacrifices of time and money to develop this talent that made them feel so proud of their son. They weren't going to give up on him just because one teacher "didn't know what he was doing."

They immediately moved into the objectification stage by refusing to accept that their son could be any less than perfect. With no regard to his feelings or needs, they began to drag him from instructor to instructor looking for one who would assure them that he was a highly talented boy. They pushed him into performance situations where he could "prove" himself, but ultimately he only embarrassed himself (and his parents).

Finally, these parents moved into the third stage of ABPD—potential abuse. They decided that the problem was caused by their son's lack of discipline and dedication. They instituted a grueling training schedule, hoping he could regain the promise he had shown as a young boy. When that didn't work and he continued to lose auditions for vocal performances, they turned their personal disappointment against their son. They blamed him for giving up, for not trying hard enough, for being weak, and so on. These parents needed their son to be an exceptional vocalist for their own gratification. His abilities and needs had nothing to do with their plans.

Are You Narcissistic and Needy?

Answer honestly the questions that follow. Every time you think deep down that the answer is yes, this should be a red flag that you may be in the ABPD parent zone.

1. Do you get angry when you feel that your child's instructor is not putting your child in the spotlight more than other kids?
2. Do you feel personally embarrassed when your child makes a public mistake? Does this embarrassment sometimes cause you to feel angry with your child and to act out that anger verbally or physically?
3. Is it necessary for your child to receive public recognition for her talents in order for it to be a truly worthwhile activity?
4. Would you be very upset if your child did not want to participate in a certain activity that would bring him (and vicariously yourself) much fame and attention?
5. Do you give up your own activities to be at a child's performances or competitions that are considered important, but do

not do so for a sibling who asks for your attendance at "unimportant" events?

6. Do you need your child's accomplishments to make you feel good?

Financially Hungry

Exceptionally talented children can make big money. Child TV, movie, and musical stars have become millionaires. Olympic athletes can make millions in commercial endorsements and exhibitions. High-achieving scholars can earn thousands and thousands of dollars in college scholarships and find remunerative careers afterwards. And we all know the financial rewards that are offered to our professional athletes. Financial gain can easily become a parent's primary driving motivation to provide years of instruction and mentoring for a talented child.

Unfortunately, when financial gain is the strongest motivating factor, the needs of the child fall to the wayside. The promise of big money can blind even the most dedicated parent. Leopold Mozart is a prime example. Toward the end of their London residence, Leopold put his children on daily public view and commented, "God willing, I shall make London my chief profit of some thousands of gulden. . . Once I leave England, I shall never see guineas again. So we must make the most of our opportunity" (quoted in Kenneson, 1998, p. 57).

Olympic gymnast Dominique Moceanu grabbed news headlines when she had a restraining order placed against her parents while she sued to achieve legal emancipation from them because of their mismanagement of her earnings. You might also remember the story of James, the high school freshman in Step One who sat the bench during baseball season. His parents were furious because they put him in this private school thinking the cost of the tuition would be offset by the athletic scholarship he would earn. They had encouraged their son's athletic talent expecting a payback that never materialized. They felt cheated, and their son consequently felt he was a failure for letting his parents down.

In another case, described in Step Two, young Brian's ambitious parents decided that their son's exceptional interest in computers could earn him a lucrative scholarship to a renowned engineering school. They moved into the stage of risky sacrifice when they invested a great deal of time and money in their son's computer hobby. They bought him the best computers, accessories, and programs, and they even flew him across the country to participate in a prestigious computer summer camp. The benefits of his achievements became the primary goal rather than a possible dividend.

They moved into the objectification stage when they let their own strong desire for a college scholarship intimidate their son into silence, making him afraid to tell his parents that he didn't want to be a computer engineer. The dollar signs blinded these parents to their child's needs and caused them to make decisions based on their own wishes and ambitions. This example typifies ABPD rooted in financial need or greed.

Are You Financially Hungry?

Answer honestly the questions that follow. Every time you think deep down that the answer is yes, this should be a red flag that you may be in the ABPD parent zone.

1. Do you invest in the development of your child's talent expecting a financial return on that investment when your child is older?
2. Have you spent money that you cannot afford on your child's talent with the rationalization that "you have to spend money to make money"?
3. Have you ever made life plans based on your child's potential income?
4. When you argue with your child over her dedication to the development of her talent, have you ever said, "Do you want a scholarship or not?"
5. Have you ever taken money your child has earned through the practice of his talent and used it for personal gain?
6. Have you controlled your child's behavior or appearance over long periods of time so that he could maintain a certain financially rewarding advertising image?

Overly Competitive Superachiever

Some people are born with a very competitive streak, but it is usually nurtured in the home as well. They live each day trying to be better than everyone around them. At work they feel constant pressure to produce more than everyone else. They stand in line at the supermarket judging how fast their line is moving compared to the other lines. Everything is a competition—who has the biggest, the most, the best. This life attitude also extends to their parenting. Their children have to be better than their peers; they have to come out on top. Life is a constant race to the finish. When overly competitive parents push their children to the front of the crowd, they are in danger of falling into ABPD traps.

Remember Mike in Step Five, who won the second-place ribbon in a track meet? His father looked at the prize and said, "When it's a first-place ribbon, then I'll get excited." Mike learned that being first was all that mattered—not how hard he tried, not how much he improved, not how he felt about his performance and the process of improvement. Overly competitive individuals view anything short of first place as a failure.

There was also the story mentioned in Step Three of the basketball coach in Massachusetts who had the backing of the team parents even though they knew he had previously been convicted of "unnatural acts with children under sixteen" and also for being "a lewd person in speech and behavior." Apparently, the competitive drive of these parents put the ability to lead a team to victory before any apparent concern about the physical or psychological safety of their children. Superachiever ABPD parents' nonverbal communication of these priorities to their children is often more powerful than any verbal statements they might make.

In Step Two we described another case of competitive drive gone awry: the grade school basketball player whose dad wanted him to play on winning teams. Matthew became a ringer, an extra player added to rosters at the last minute when a team needed a talented backup. Having invested much time, money, and effort to this cause, Matthew's father had objectified his son. It didn't matter that Matthew was not able to enjoy team camaraderie, loyalty, or social interaction in these situations. The goal was to be on a winning team, no matter what the financial or emotional cost. In Matthew's father's game book, the most important thing about competing was to win.

This competitive attitude is fostered in the general public, in professional sports, and with many "career" children. This seems certainly to be so in the case of media mogul Ted Turner. Turner is the founder of CNN, owner of the Atlanta Braves, almost Olympic yachtsman, America's Cup winner, and founder of the Goodwill Games, among many other things. He reports following his father Ed Turner's dictum to "always set your goals higher than what you can achieve in your lifetime." This advice might have given Turner pause to reflect when his father shot himself at the age of fifty-three "because he'd already exceeded his dreams and couldn't reorient himself to seek out other mountains to climb." Perhaps for this reason Ted Turner's ambition is nothing short of "saving the world." He says, "I'm sure that it's not healthy to be a super achiever or to be super driven. I think the happiest people are those who have more normal levels of ambition and drive" (quoted in Lieber, 2000, pp. C1, C2).

Are You an Overly Competitive Superachiever?

Answer honestly the questions that follow. Every time you think deep down that the answer is yes, this should be a red flag that you may be in the ABPD parent zone.

1. Do you overtly or secretly rejoice when your child's rivals are injured or fall by the wayside during a competition, or when their parents suffer some loss that affects their child?
2. Do you verbally abuse your child's coaches, referees, umpires, or instructors?
3. Do you ask your child, "Did you win?" before even thinking to ask, "How did you do?"
4. Do you tell your child or behave as if "winning isn't everything—it's the only thing"?
5. Do you feel angry, empty, or betrayed when your child doesn't come in "first"?
6. Do you encourage your child to beat out teammates or peers, even in practice?
7. Do you base your decisions about your child's education or competitive plans only on her chances of winning rather than

on longer-term developmental reasons, such as her exposure to a good competitive field or venue for objective competition?

Frustrated Could-a-Been Champion

It is not unreasonable for parents to have high hopes and dreams for their children—up to a certain point. Adults' dreams and goals that have been dashed by time, ill luck, and injury can come alive again with the birth of a child; they also open the door to an ABPD situation. "I didn't make it to the big leagues," a dad will say, "but my son will," regardless of the son's desires or capabilities. Because these parents have been disappointed or thwarted in the course of their own lives, they need their children to achieve the lost goals for them.

This is one theme of the famous musical *Gypsy*. During a very powerful moment in the story, the mother sings a song that confesses her feelings that the success should have been hers because she was better than her daughter, but life is so unfair in these kinds of things. Whether the child becomes successful or falls short of the top, a parent's displaced personal dreams can cause many families to fall into ABPD traps.

In Step Four, we met a twelve-year-old boy who excelled in the martial arts. His dad had wanted to continue his own training as a young man, but family obligations interfered. Now he was determined that his son would do what he could not, even if that meant dedicating all his time to his son's practice and competition schedule while ignoring the needs and accomplishments of his daughter. Having his son achieve his own lost dream was all that mattered to this father.

Another case of disappointed dreams involved a young dancer named Clara Woods. Clara's mother had studied to be a professional dancer, but ended her short stage career by opening a small-town dance studio. She raised her daughter in the ballet studio from the moment she could walk, expecting that this child would find the spotlight that had eluded Clara's mother in her own life. When Clara grew and her physique turned out to be more like that of her dad—large, lumbering, and a bit uncoordinated—Clara's mother was so consumed by her visions of regaining lost stardom that she objectified her child. She was unable to put the reality of her daughter's life before her own dreams. She forced Clara into performance situations that caused her embarrassment and humiliation in front of her peers.

Are You a Frustrated Could-a-Been Champion?

Answer honestly the questions that follow. Every time you think deep down that the answer is yes, this should be a red flag that you may be in the ABPD parent zone.

1. Is your child deeply involved in an activity that *you* excelled in as a child?
2. Do you often dwell on the fact that you did not reach your goal or potential in this activity?
3. Have you been telling your child since he was born that he would make you proud by doing what you could not do?
4. Do you get angry or furious when your child refuses to take advantage of your experience and learn from your mistakes?
5. Do you sometimes feel jealous of the opportunities that await your child?
6. Do you try to hog the limelight, competing with the success your child experiences?

The Routine Rationalizer

Some parents see their children in potentially harmful situations but remain quiet, even oblivious, for long periods of time. Some allow a spouse or coach to mistreat their children while they remain passive and uninvolved. Others fear that their objections may keep the child from competing at the top, such as the gymnasts' parents who continue to send their children to Bela Karolyi after many cases of publicized negative coaching techniques. They turn a blind eye and ignore the inherent danger or rationalize that it is character building. They live in denial, hoping the problem isn't really as bad as it looks. When parents use plausible deniability as an excuse for not carrying out their parental obligation to protect their children, they have fallen into a dangerous ABPD trap.

In Step Six, we saw the father of a high school football player who shut his eyes to his son's suspected steroid abuse in the belief that if "everybody" else was doing it, his son deserved an equal advantage.

We have seen the parents of a gymnast and the parents of a dancer ignore the signs of eating disorders in their young daughters. They rationalize by saying, "If she wants or needs to be thinner in order to compete with the best, that's her decision; she's mature, and there's nothing we can do about it. She can quit any time."

In Step Three, we saw parents who handed over their parental authority to their children's instructors. Maria's figure skating instructor told her she could skip school to get in more hours of practice. Hal's math tutor gave him certain herbal supplements and untried "cognitive enhancers" to improve brainpower. Kathleen's fencing coach registered her for a residential summer camp. The parents didn't want to upset the child's instructors and so ignored the situation.

We have seen a father who turned a deaf ear to members of his daughter's swim team who warned him that the coach possibly was sexually abusing his daughter. He worried that a confrontation would jeopardize his daughter's future on the team. After much soul searching, he concluded that it was best to remain silent!

The question each of these parents needs to answer honestly is, Best for whom? In most cases, the truth points to the parents' needs and interests, not the child's.

Are You a Routine Rationalizer?

Answer honestly the questions that follow. Every time you think deep down that the answer is yes, this should be a red flag that you may be in the ABPD parent zone.

1. Do you often let your child's instructor make important decisions for your child?
2. Do you brush off your child's complaints about an instructor with such comments as "Come on, honey, he's the best. He knows what he's doing!"?
3. Do you stay uninvolved in your child's training program, assuming the instructor knows best?
4. Do you allow your spouse to exhibit ABPD behaviors without interference?

5. Do you ignore dangerous warning signs for fear that investigation may interfere with the development of your child's potential or that her powerful instructor will drop her as a pupil?
6. Are you afraid to confront your spouse about her verbal abuse of your child because you fear it may then be turned toward you?
7. Have you ever let your child live with an instructor?

Untangling the Roots of Achievement by Proxy Distortion

ABPD traps are rooted in all the parenting types described in the preceding sections. Parents will actively encourage or allow their children to be used and abused in the pursuit of success for one, several, or all of these reasons. Parenting traits are a complex entanglement of many needs, desires, and realities. In order to encourage yet protect our children, we need to be able to recognize the symptoms of these traits in our own actions and underlying needs. We need to step back and look at the child as a whole person—not just the vessel of a singular talent but as a person with developmental needs, hopes, dreams, and desires independent of our own lives. We hope they will live on long after we are gone and will have within them the knowledge that their parents loved them for who they are as a person, not for what they could successfully accomplish. This is the greatest gift we can give to our high-achieving children.

Encourage and Support

You will be able to encourage and support your high-achieving athletes, scholars, and performing artists if you keep in mind the seven guidelines of appropriately involved parenting that we described in "From Benign to Abusive" in Part One. We repeat the guidelines here; we suggest that you make a copy of them and keep the list handy and visible. Check every decision you make regarding the development of your child's talent against this list.

Guidelines for Healthy Involvement

- Guideline 1: Parents should acknowledge the child as a unique individual with his or her own separate physical and psychological attributes.

- Guideline 2: Parents should be able to recognize the child's psychological and physical needs and then make and prioritize decisions based on these requirements rather than on their own wishes, ambitions, and fantasies.
- Guideline 3: Parents should be able to distinguish between their own feelings of anger and disappointment (as well as their pride and pleasure) and the child's feelings; they should not justify their actions by projecting their own feelings onto the child.
- Guideline 4: Children should never feel that parental love is contingent on winning or excelling in any one educational, sporting, career, or social endeavor.
- Guideline 5: Parents must retain the power to make parental decisions (although this should not be confused with being an autocratic parent, as described in this chapter). It is crucial that parents make tough—even courageous and unpopular—but developmentally appropriate judgments for the child.
- Guideline 6: Parents should encourage developmentally appropriate independence, autonomy, and decision-making skills in their children. They should not, however, hide behind that independence when important, even critical, decisions are to be made.
- Guideline 7: Social and financial benefits of the child's achievements should be a *dividend* rather than a primary (or even a disguised primary) goal for the adult. (In other words, always be a parent *first* and an agent and career manager second.)

Frequently reviewing these guidelines will remind you that your very special child is not you, although she carries half your genes. She lives in a world that you can shape but cannot own. Your child's future accomplishments can be encouraged but not dictated. Your goal now should be to help, support, and inspire your child through your own example to explore, reach, strive, and experience pleasure, joy, and success in this life that is so precious and fragile.

Epilogue

The dilemmas of keeping kids out front without kicking them from behind are inherent in ambitious parents' blueprints or fantasies for their children's future. There will continue to be parents who exploit their children for selfish purposes. There will always be parents who stand on the sidelines yelling and berating every wrong move their children make. There will continue to be parents who push their children beyond their developmental capabilities in the hope of a financial payoff down the road. And there will be good parents who for extremely subtle but self-serving reasons will undermine their children's future while driving them "altruistically" toward success in areas in which the children's talents do not lie. Unfortunately, even long after this book is published many more families will be torn apart by the tension and strain of ABPD-related situations.

But it is our humble hope that this book will begin to reduce these numbers. We hope to draw greater attention to the qualitative degradation of childhood that has become commonplace in this generation. We hope that more and more parents, teachers, mentors, and coaches will stand back and realize that their children are more likely to achieve their full, multidimensional potential when they are encouraged and protected rather than pushed and bullied into high performance. It is our hope that after reading this book you will always remember to love your children first and foremost for who they are, not for what they do.

References

ABC. *Politically Incorrect*. [http://abc.go.com/pi/forum/xscripts/199111 2.html]. Nov. 12, 1999.

Adato, A. "Solo in the City." *Los Angeles Times Magazine,* Dec. 5, 1999, p. 16.

American Academy of Child and Adolescent Psychiatry. "Teen Suicide." [http://www.aacap.org/factsfam/suicide.htm]. Nov. 1998.

Associated Press. "Karolyi to End Long, Controversial Career." Olympic Features Page. [http:www.nando.net/newsroom/ap/oth/1996/oth/oly/feat/archive/072696/oly666159.html].

Baum, A. L. "Young Females in the Athletic Arena." In I. R. Tofler (ed.), *Sport Psychiatry: Child and Adolescent Psychiatric Clinics of North America.* Vol. 7. Philadelphia: Saunders, Oct. 1998.

Begel, D. and Burton, R. W. (eds.). *Sport Psychiatry, Theory and Practice.* New York: Norton, 2000.

Bloom, B. S. (ed.). *Developing Talent in Young People.* New York: Ballantine, 1985.

Bronner, E. "For '99 College Applicants, Stiffest Competition Ever." *New York Times,* June 12, 1999, pp. A1, A11.

Cohen, W. "Prosecution Slap Shot." *U.S. News and World Report,* Feb. 7, 2000, *128*(5), 26.

Coleman, J. "Killing of Japanese Toddler Blamed on Education System." *The Record,* Dec. 3, 1999, p. A33.

DiSalvo, J., and DiGeronimo, T. *College Admissions for the High School Athlete.* New York: Facts on File, 2000.

Elkind, D. "Authority of the Brain." *Journal of Developmental and Behavioral Pediatrics,* December 1999, *20,* 432–433.

Elkind, D. *The Hurried Child.* Malibu, Calif.: Perseus Press, 1989.

Elliott, H. "Talk Is Cheap on Sexual Misconduct." *Los Angeles Times,* Jan. 7, 1997, p. C-8.

Eminson, M. and Postlewaite, R. J. *Munchausen Syndrome by Proxy Abuse, a Practical Approach.* Oxford: Butterworth-Heinemann, 2000.

Engh, F. *Why Johnny Hates Sports.* Garden City Park, N.Y.: Avery, 1999.

"Epic Battle for the Heart of a Child Prodigy." *20/20.* Dec. 6, 1998.

Escarti, A., Roberts, G., Cervello, E., and Guzman, J. "Adolescent Goal Orientations and the Perception of Criteria of Success Used by Significant Others." *International Journal of Sports Psychology,* 1999, *30,* 309–324.

Farragher, T. "Concord Teen's Success Something to Brag About." *Boston Globe,* Apr. 18, 1999, p. B1.

Fisher, R. B. *Musical Prodigies: Masters at an Early Age.* New York: Association Press, 1973.

Gaa, G., and others. "Prevalence of Anabolic Steroid Use Among Illinois High School Students." *Journal of Athletic Training,* 1994, *29,* 216–222.

Gleick, J. *Genius: The Life and Science of Richard Feynman.* New York: Pantheon Books, 1992.

Gold, S., and Weber, T. "Youth Sports Grind Is Tough on Body, Spirit." *Los Angeles Times,* Feb. 28, 2000, p. A1.

Goldsmith, S. "Kaiser's Dirty Secret." *New Times Los Angeles,* Dec. 9, 1999, p. 10.

Joravsky, B. *Hoop Dreams: A True Story of Hardship and Triumph.* New York: Harper Collins, 1996.

Kann, L., and others. "Youth Risk Behavior Surveillance: United States, 1995." *MMWR Centers for Disease Control Surveillance Summary,* 1996, *45,* 1–84.

Kenneson, C. *Musical Prodigies: Perilous Journeys, Remarkable Lives.* Portland, Oreg.: Amadeus Press, 1998.

Klawans, H. *Why Michael Couldn't Hit.* New York: Avon Books, 1998.

Kogan, J. *Nothing but the Best: The Struggle for Perfection at the Juilliard School.* New York: Random House, 1987.

Libman, S. "Adult Participation in Youth Sports." In I. R. Tofler (ed.), *Sport Psychiatry: Child and Adolescent Psychiatric Clinics of North America.* Vol. 7. Philadelphia: Saunders, Oct. 1998.

Lieber, J. "Turner Still Thinking Big." *USA Today,* Feb. 17, 2000, pp. C1–C2.

"Life in Romania, Texas." *Newsweek,* Oct. 25, 1999, p. 73.

McNamee, M. J., and Parry, S. J. (eds.). *Ethics and Sport.* London: Routlidge, 1998.

Meadow, R. "What Is, and What Is Not, 'Munchausen Syndrome by Proxy?'" *Archives of Diseases of Children,* 1995, *72,* 534–538.

Miller, A. "The Drama of the Gifted Child and the Psycho-Analyst's Narcissistic Disturbance." *International Journal of Psychoanalysis,* 1979, *60,* 47–58.

Murphy, S. *The Cheers and the Tears.* San Francisco, Calif.: Jossey-Bass, 1999.

Nack, W., and Yaeger, D. "Every Parent's Nightmare." *Sports Illustrated,* Sept. 13, 1999, *91*(10), 40–53.

Oestreich, J. "Juilliard Tries to Nurture Well-Tempered Artists." *New York Times,* May 23, 1999, pp. A1, 27.

Ogilvie, B. C., Tofler, I. R., Conroy, D. E., and Drell, M. J. "Comprehending Role Conflicts in the Coaching of Children, Adolescents, and Young Adults." In I. R. Tofler (ed.), *Sport Psychiatry: Child and Adolescent Psychiatric Clinics of North America.* Vol. 7. Philadelphia: Saunders, Oct. 1998.

Packard, V. *Our Endangered Children.* New York: Little, Brown, 1983.

Pillemer, F. G., and Micheli, L. J. "Psychological Considerations in Youth Sports." *Clinics in Sports Medicine,* July 1988, p. 7.

Radford, J. *Child Prodigies and Exceptional Early Achievers.* New York: Free Press, 1990.

Renzulli, J. "The Three-Ring Conception of Giftedness." In S. M. Baum, S. M. Reis, and L. R. Maxfield (eds.), *Nurturing the Gifts and Talents of Primary Grade Students.* Mansfield Center, Conn.: Creative Learning Press, 1998. Available on-line at [http://sp.uconn.edu/~nrcgt/sem/semart13.html].

Romano, B. "Another Bandleader Faces Sex Allegation." *San Jose Mercury News,* 1995, p. 1A.

"Secrets of the SAT. Interviews: Robert Sternberg." *Frontline.* [http://www.pbs.org/wgbh/pages/frontline/shows/sats/interviews/sternberg]. Oct. 5, 1999.

Seligman, M. *The Optimistic Child.* New York: Harper Perennial Library, 1996.

Seligson, T. "I Wanted This So Bad, It Hurt." *Parade Magazine,* Mar. 5, 2000, pp. 4, 5.

Sports Illustrated. Tiger Woods: The Making of a Champion. New York: Simon & Schuster, 1996.

Stern, I. *Isaac Stern: My First Seventy-Nine Years.* New York: Knopf, 1999.

Stryer, B. K., Tofler, I. R., and Lapchick, R. "A Developmental Overview of Child and Youth Sports in Society." In I. R. Tofler (ed.), *Sport Psychiatry: Child and Adolescent Psychiatric Clinics of North America.* Vol. 7. Philadelphia: Saunders, Oct. 1998.

Subotnik, R. "Talent Developed: Conversations with Masters in the Arts and Sciences." *Journal for the Education of the Gifted,* 1997, *20*(3), 306–317.

"Through the Stardust." *Vanity Fair,* May 1999, pp. 146–150, 196–198.

Tofler, I. R. "Parental and Adult Professional Gain from Exceptional Children: Achievement by Proxy." In Eminson, M. and Postlewaite, R. J., *Munchausen Syndrome by Proxy Abuse, a Practical Approach.* Oxford, Butterworth-Heinemann, 2000: 215–230.

Tofler, I. R., Knapp, P. K., Drell, M. J. "The Achievement by Proxy Spectrum in Youth Sports: Historical Perspective and Clinical Approach to Pressured and High-Achieving Children and Adolescents." In I. R. Tofler (ed.), *Sport Psychiatry: Child and Adolescent Psychiatric Clinics of North America.* Vol. 7, 803–820. Philadelphia: Saunders, Oct. 1998.

Tofler, I. R., Knapp, P. K., Drell, M. J. "The 'Achievement by Proxy' Spectrum: Recognition and Clinical Response to Pressured and High-Achieving Children and Adolescents." *Journal of American Academy of Child and Adolescent Psychiatry,* Feb. 1999, *38:*2.

Tofler, I. R., Stryker, B. K., Micheli, L. J., Herman L. R. "Physical and Emotional Problems of Elite Female Gymnasts." *New England Journal of Medicine,* 1996, *335:* 281–283.

Weissinger, E., and others. "Weight Loss Behavior in High School Wrestling: Wrestler and Parent Perceptions." *Pediatric Exercise Science,* 1991, *3,* 64–73.

The Authors

Ian Tofler, M.D., inaugural Chair of the Sport Psychiatry Committee of the American Academy of Child and Adolescent Psychiatry, is a child and adolescent psychiatrist in private practice who also works with neglected and abused children at Hollygrove Children's Home in Los Angeles. Actively involved with research and publication in the area of elite children and their psychological problems, he edited the first book in the new field of sport psychiatry, and is the co-originator of the term "Achievement By Proxy" Behavior and Distortion (ABPD). He lives with his wife and three small children in Los Angeles, California.

Theresa DiGeronimo, M. Ed., is adjunct professor of English and communications at William Paterson University of New Jersey. She is the coauthor of *How to Talk to Your Kids About Really Important Things*, *How to Talk to Teens About Really Important Things*, and dozens of other parenting and children's books. She is the mother of three children and lives in Hawthorne, New Jersey.

Index